WRITERS' WORKSHOP SERIES

How to teach writing across the curriculum at key stage 1

SUE PALMER

David Fulton Publishers

David Fulton Publishers Ltd
The Chiswick Centre, 414 Chiswick High Road, London W4 5TF

www.fultonpublishers.co.uk
www.onestopeducation.co.uk

David Fulton Publishers is a division of Granada Learning, part of the ITV plc.

First published in 2003
10 9 8 7 6 5 4

Note: the right of Sue Palmer to be identified as the author of this work has been asserted by her in accordance with the Copyright, Design and Patents Act 1998

Copyright © Sue Palmer 2003

British Library Cataloguing in Publication Data
A catalogue record for this book is available from the British Library.

ISBN 1 85346 919 X

Also available in the **Writers' Workshop Series:**

How to teach story writing at key stage 1   Pie Corbett   ISBN 1 85346 916 5
How to teach poetry writing at key stage 1   Michaela Morgan   ISBN 1 85346 918 1

Cover design by Phil Barker
Cover photograph by John Redman
Illustrations by Martin Cater
Designed and typeset by FiSH Books, London
Printed and bound in Great Britain

Contents

Acknowledgements

This book owes its existence to the many teachers throughout the UK who heard about 'skeletons' on my literacy in-service courses, tried them out in the classroom and reported back. I am greatly indebted to them for their interest, enthusiasm, generosity and wisdom.

Thanks are also due to the National Literacy Strategy, which sponsored me to investigate the use of skeletons in junior classes, and to David Fulton Publishers for commissioning an earlier book *How to Teach Writing Across the Curriculum at Key Stage 2*. This work made me desperately keen to know how skeletons would work with younger children, and increased my focus on the significance of speaking and listening as a precursor of any writing activity.

The opportunity to find out more was offered by Jeremy Sugden, editor of *Child Education* magazine, who let me research and write a series of articles on using skeletons in Key Stage 1. Several of the case studies in *How to Teach Writing Across the Curriculum at Key Stage 1* are based on these articles; others have been generously provided by teachers I met during in-service travels.

Finally, I would like to thank the children of the Abbey School, Wybourne Primary School, East Dene School, Sacred Heart Catholic Primary School, Comin Infants School, Roskear Primary School, Yew Tree Primary School and Totley Primary School for providing the many lovely examples of work. This is by far the best way of illustrating how to teach – and learn – cross-curricular writing skills.

Sue Palmer

The publishers would like to thank the staff and pupils of Roskear School, Cambourne, for their help in arranging the photo shoot at which the picture on the cover of this book was taken and Clive Felton, head teacher of Weston Park Primary School, Bristol, for permission to use the illustration of a spelling mat on p. 10.

Introduction

Teaching children to write involves developing a wide range of skills – handwriting, phonic encoding, spelling, sentence construction, choice of vocabulary, text organisation, and many more – while at the same time helping them control and orchestrate these skills in the momentous act of composition.

It is a mammoth task, perhaps the most difficult in the whole of primary education, but an incredibly worthwhile one. The ability to write frees children to explore and express their ideas; to communicate what they think and know; to record – and, through recording, take ownership of – all that they learn. This book concentrates on the development of factual cross-curricular writing, and looks at how we can lay the foundations for effective writing in a range of non-fiction forms and styles.

Cross-curricular literacy teaching

Foundation and Key Stage 1 teachers have traditionally used a cross-curricular approach, but in recent years this has been less easy to achieve. In England and Wales, the introduction of the National Curriculum led to increasing compartmentalisation of subject teaching. More recently, in England the National Literacy Strategy (NLS) with its highly structured 'Literacy Hour' has often meant that reading and writing are taught in isolation from the rest of the curriculum. Schools in Scotland, Wales and Northern Ireland which introduced 'ring-fenced time' and a continuum of teaching objectives for literacy have also found it more difficult to make the links.

There are great advantages to this more structured approach to literacy, especially the fact that a clear continuum of teaching objectives ensures systematic coverage of all those skills, subskills and concepts children need to become readers and writers. But when literacy objectives are covered in isolation – without some sort of meaningful context to bring them to life – teaching and learning can become very arid. What's the point of learning to write unless you have real reasons to commit your thoughts to paper, and relevant content to write about?

Fortunately, now that the curricular and literacy initiatives of the last decade or so have begun to 'bed down', the educational ethos is beginning to loosen up. Teachers in England are no longer required to stick to the Literacy Hour's rigid '15,15,20,10' structure – indeed, many publications no longer refer to the Hour, but to the 'daily literacy lesson'. Literacy gurus everywhere are looking again at integrating reading and writing into children's wider learning. This is certainly the message of the National Literacy Strategy's book *Developing Early Writing*, which describes a number of cross-curricular projects, and of the Qualifications and Curriculum Authority (QCA), which now includes literacy links along with each of its schemes of work (see Teacher resources, Appendix 5).

Some aspects of literacy teaching will necessarily remain decontextualised – most word-level work at Key Stage 1, for instance, does not fit comfortably into a cross-curricular context as it is concerned with the patterns and shapes of language. However, now that teachers are more confident of sentence and text-level literacy objectives, many aspects of reading comprehension and writing composition can be safely integrated without losing the rigour of objectives-based teaching.

Through ensuring structured coverage of the objectives *and* real, stimulating contexts for reading and writing, we can make literacy learning more meaningful while, at the same time, enhancing learning in other subject areas. Reading about the topic under discussion and writing about what they have learned helps children to consolidate their understanding. And, from a practical point of view, the more links that can be made in a crowded curriculum, the better for everyone's sanity!

How to teach cross-curricular writing at Key Stage 1

This book is divided into three parts:

- **Teaching strategies**, which covers the 'how and why' of teaching cross-curricular writing
- **Teaching practice** – ten case studies of teachers' work from around England and Wales, showing how these strategies have been put into practice in real classrooms
- **Teaching materials** – a collection of texts, photocopiable sheets and teaching notes which provide starting points for teaching cross-curricular writing through a variety of projects.

Further information on the skills which underlie writing success is provided in Appendices 1 to 3.

Teaching strategies

1 Teaching writing in Foundation and Key Stage 1

In the last few years, a great deal of attention has been paid to the skills involved when children write and to the best ways to teach them. This book is based on a variety of pedagogical techniques, developed by teachers and researchers around the world, and popularised in British schools by the National Literacy Strategy and similar initiatives in Scotland, Wales and Ireland. The terminology used is generally that adopted by the NLS.

Skills development

It is now widely accepted that, in the early stages, children's ability to write is underpinned by the development of the skills of phonics, spelling and handwriting. In order to write a word down, a child must be able to hear it, translate it into the appropriate sequence of symbols, and transcribe those symbols onto the page. Some common English words (such as *one* and *they*) have irregular spellings and must be recognised, remembered and transcribed as wholes but, with a reasonable grasp of phonics, most words can be transcribed phonetically.

Although this book is not specifically concerned with the development of these writing subskills, it is essential to point out that phonic knowledge, handwriting and whole-word recognition of significant irregular words are critical to writing success. These skills and knowledge must be developed in a structured and systematic way alongside meaningful cross-curricular literacy activities, and teachers should take every opportunity to demonstrate to children how they are integrated in the act of writing. Some suggestions for the teaching of phonics and handwriting in Foundation and Key Stage 1, based on advice from HMI, the NLS and on observation of successful practice, are included in Appendix 1 and Appendix 2.

Once children have begun to develop a grasp of these word-level skills, they must also begin to develop awareness of the grammatical elements involved in writing. This means teaching another layer of subskills, concerned with the construction and punctuation of sentences, and ways of varying language use for different purposes. Sentence-level knowledge is best introduced through the context of shared reading – discussing how authors have achieved their effects – and supplemented by games and activities to help children understand the concepts. In Shared Writing, the teacher can then demonstrate how this knowledge is applied during the act of composition. Background information on grammar teaching in Key Stage 1 is provided in Appendix 3.

Shared writing

The technique of Shared Writing is the main vehicle through which teachers can demonstrate to children how word- and sentence-level subskills are brought together in the act of writing. The NLS suggests that it should involve three main types of activity: Demonstration, Scribing and Supported Writing (see opposite page).

These three types of teaching are admirably demonstrated on the NLS video *Developing Early Writing*, which was distributed to all primary schools in England in 2001 (see Teacher resources, Appendix 5).

Guided writing

After the highly directed experience of Shared Writing, children need opportunities to try out the process for themselves, writing independently or with a degree of teacher supervision. To a large extent, children's developmental level (see box on p. 8) will dictate how much they can achieve when writing independently, and teaching must take account of this.

DEMONSTRATION	SCRIBING	SUPPORTED WRITING
The teacher models the process of writing for the children, beginning with oral composition of each sentence. The teacher writes the demonstration text on the board or flip-chart, and keeps up a constant commentary on what s/he is doing and why. This should include explicit demonstration of how to segment and blend words to write them phonetically. This demonstrates to children exactly how ideas get out of someone's head and on to the page. It also demonstrates exactly what the child should be doing and thinking when trying to write independently.	Scribing is a way of involving the class in the composition of shared writing. The teacher invites the children to contribute ideas, forms of words, alternative constructions, etc. Children should be given the opportunity to talk with a partner for a few seconds, to discuss and choose the best word, phrase or sentence. (See advice on paired work on page 19.) The teacher chooses the most successful and says why s/he likes it. This form of words is integrated into the demonstration, with the teacher still keeping up the commentary.	Every so often, the teacher asks pairs of pupils to work on a section of text together. The best supported writing tasks involve putting one or more of the day's learning objectives into immediate practice. It is helpful to display a visual reminder of an agreed procedure for supported writing (e.g. see page 20). Otherwise, valuable time can be lost reminding pupils orally, and this interferes with their auditory memory of the specific writing task. When pupils give feedback, the procedure continues as for 'Scribing'.

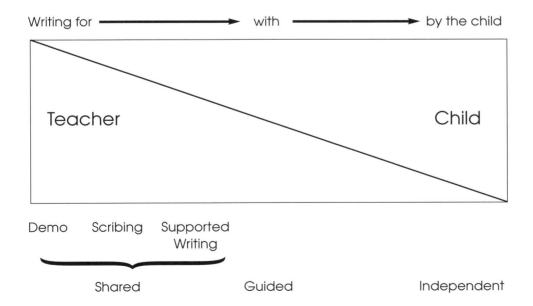

Writing for ⟶ with ⟶ by the child

Teacher   Child

Demo   Scribing   Supported Writing

Shared   Guided   Independent

A combination of Shared, Guided and Independent Writing provides many different levels of support. In Demonstration Writing, the teacher has complete control of the process: this control is then gradually handed over to the children so that, during Independent Writing, they are empowered to write for themselves.

Children's developmental level in emergent writing is directly affected by appropriate skills teaching at other times during the school day. Good structured phonics teaching, along with sensitively managed development of handwriting skills, ensures that children have the data and physical control they need to write. Without it, they will develop slowly or not at all; with it, their developmental progress can be greatly accelerated. See Appendices 1 and 2.

In the Foundation stage, as children acquire basic phonic and handwriting skills, the distinction between Independent and Guided Writing is often blurred. Indeed, the NLS recognises that in Reception classes (children aged 4–5), most children are not ready for whole-class teaching:

- very young children often need individual attention when attempting to write, either from the teacher or from classroom helpers, and the spread of ability is usually such that grouping would be impossible
- the first groupings to emerge will benefit most from small-scale Shared Writing sessions as described in the chart on page 7.

As the children mature and the number of participants in Shared Writing sessions grows, it should be possible to identify smaller Guided Writing groups (about six children of roughly similar ability). The NLS suggests that, by the end of the Reception year, most children in most schools should be able to participate in Shared, Guided and Independent Writing.

Guided Writing offers the teacher an opportunity to home in more closely on specific children's needs than is possible in the Shared session. There are three major advantages to working with Guided Writing groups rather than with individual children:

- In a group situation, there is less temptation to focus too heavily on a particular child and thus offer more support or direction than is helpful. Too much 'help' makes children over-dependent on adult intervention. Within a group, the teacher can focus in general on the teaching objective, rather than any individual child.
- While it is obviously helpful to offer selective prompting about basic skills at point of need – at the very moment when children are writing – it is difficult to achieve a sensitive balance between
  - guiding children towards correctness
  - encouraging them to think for themselves and 'take risks' in their writing.

Over-emphasis on correctness is more likely to inhibit writing development than to aid it. In a group it is easier to point out errors in a more general way, without directing the spotlight at any one individual.

- Children benefit infinitely more from praise for what they achieve than from having attention drawn to their mistakes. In a group, the teacher can single out individual pupils for praise and thus, incidentally, raise awareness among all group members about what is deserving of praise.

On the whole, Guided Writing at Key Stage 1 is usually based on ability groups, although by Year 2 it may sometimes be more appropriate occasionally to form 'ad hoc' groups, to tackle particular aspects of writing. If the majority of an ability group is secure on, say, capital letters for proper names, it would be wasteful to make that the focus of an entire session for them. When a writing task arises that provides a good vehicle for reteaching the topic, the teacher can create a one-off group of children from across the class who need help with that aspect of sentence-level work.

Independent writing

As children develop as writers, they need more and more opportunities to write independently, without adult intervention. By the middle of Year 1, it should be possible in most classrooms to arrange at least two sessions (of about twenty minutes) per week specifically dedicated to Independent Writing, during which the teacher works with a Guided Writing group. Such sessions will generally follow directly after a Shared Writing session, so that children have watched the teacher model the relevant writing behaviour before going off to try it for themselves. By Year 2, there will be many further occasions, throughout the curriculum, when children have opportunities to write independently.

Independent Writing is the children's opportunity to put all that data, learned elsewhere in the literacy curriculum, into practice – what the NLS calls 'orchestrating the skills'. A number of practical considerations can make the difference between successful and unsuccessful independent work:

- There should be well-established classroom procedures for obvious problems like checking on a spelling – children should be well trained in these procedures and should not need to keep checking with the teacher.

Have a go!

When you are writing, **have a go** at spelling words.

When you've finished, read your work.

If a spelling looks wrong, try to put it right.

- Every care should be taken to avoid obvious 'flashpoints' in the classroom. For instance, it is often better if easily distractable children do not sit together – this may well mean that members of the less able group do not sit at the same table for independent work.
- It is often enlightening to spend a day or two every so often observing independent work, rather than taking a group. If children are told that the teacher is still out of bounds on these occasions, they soon forget they are being watched, and one can learn much about classroom culture. On the basis of this research, it may be possible to make adjustments to the organisation of furniture, equipment and so on that will lead to calmer behaviour. The teacher can also use his/her observations as the basis of a discussion with the class to negotiate classroom rules and procedures – children with 'ownership' of the rules are usually more interested in keeping them.
- Children's independent work improves when they know exactly what they are expected to do, and what the teacher is looking for. Independent writing should therefore follow a Shared Writing session, and all children should attempt the same task, with different levels of scaffolding for different ability groups. Objectives and outcomes should be clearly described (the less able the child, the more specific should be the expected outcomes).

An important aspect of independent writing is children's confidence. If they are over-worried about correctness and afraid to take risks, they will not take full advantage of the opportunity to use the skills you have been teaching them. It is only by actively using data that learners truly internalise it, so it is essential that the prevailing ethos during Independent Writing time is 'have a go' – and that children feel free to use their newly acquired skills at the level appropriate to them.

Teachers should be aware of each child's potential (see notes on developmental writing in Appendix 1) and, on the whole, one's response to errors in Independent Writing should be to ask oneself what further teaching is required (or, more likely, what revision of previous teaching).

As time goes on, however, some children's development – particularly in terms of phonic and/or handwriting skills – lags behind that of their peers. Teachers naturally (and very rightly) worry that the 'have a go' ethos is not always helpful to these children. If, for instance, a child in Year 2 repeatedly writes *sed* instead of *said*, there is a real danger that s/he will over-learn the incorrect spelling, which it will be very difficult to eradicate in the future.

These children themselves sometimes find advice to 'have a go' frustrating. If the mismatch between what they want to achieve and what they are capable of achieving is too great, writing will become an increasingly onerous and unattractive task. As well as slow skills development, the

a	b	c	d	e	f	g	h	i	j	k	l	m	n	o	p	q	r	s
about	back	call	did		first	girl	half		jump		last	made	name	of	people		ran	said
after	ball	called	do		for	go	have		just		laugh	make	new	off	pull		right	saw
again	be	came	don't		from	going	help				like	many	next	old	push			school
all	because	can't	door			good	her				little	may	night	once	put			see
another	been	come	down				here				live	more	not	one				seen
away	boy	could					home				lived	much	now	or				she
	brother						house				love	must		our				should
	by						how							out				sister
														over				so
																		some

t	u	v	w	x	y	z
take	under	very	want		you	
than	us		water		your	
that			way			
their			were			
them			what			
there			when			
these			where			
three			who			
time			will			
too			with			
took			would			
two						
they						

TOPIC WORDS

A writing mat, showing irregularly spelled key words. These can be provided on A3-size laminated cards for children requiring extra support in spelling (see p. 11).

teacher then has to deal with a steady spiral of poor motivation, lack of application and, all too often, deteriorating behaviour patterns.

It is therefore very important to identify slow developers as early as possible, try to work out the reason behind their difficulties, and provide appropriate 'catch-up' support. This requires the involvement of the Special Needs Coordinator and is beyond the scope of this book. On a day-to-day level, however, teachers should always try to ensure that, during Independent Writing, provision is made to support such children through specific areas of difficulty.

For instance, the *sed/said* problem can be addressed by providing children with 'writing mats' – laminated A3 cards on which irregularly spelled key words are provided in alphabetical lists, and which they can lean upon to write. The children can then be advised to 'have a go' like the rest of the class, with a simple proviso: 'BUT... if it's on the mat, copy it'.

The National Literacy Strategy refers to such specific support as 'scaffolding', and advises that teachers try to 'scaffold out' as many potential problems as possible, so that each child is able to engage with a writing task in a way that ensures active mental processing at a level likely to encourage learning. This is considerably easier said than done, but worth pursuing. Empowering children to 'orchestrate the skills' for themselves – at whatever level is appropriate for the individual learner – is the most likely way of ensuring successful development of writing skills.

And whenever they get something right – praise them!

Preparation for writing

In describing the system the NLS devised for the teaching of writing before considering children's preparation to write, I have been guilty – as was the Literacy Strategy – of putting the cart before the horse. Children cannot, of course, be expected to write unless they have something to write about. Nor can they commit ideas to paper unless they have adequate command of the English language to express those ideas in the first place.

While the recent emphasis on literacy skills in primary schools has yielded many positive results, too great a focus on 'pencil and paper work' has often meant these two rather obvious points have been neglected. In England, the Literacy Strategy was well into its third year before sufficient attention was paid to preparation for writing. However, in its publication *Developing Early Writing* (2001), the Strategy clearly advised that all writing activities should be preceded by *planning* and *talk for writing*.

These aspects are of particular importance for cross-curricular work, since they relate to the way in which children:

- internalise information covered in another area of the curriculum and organise it into an appropriate form for writing
- internalise knowledge about the language of writing, acquired through Shared and Guided Reading, and learn to manipulate it orally before beginning to write.

Now that I have summed up some important aspects of the writing 'cart', the rest of this book will be concerned with the two 'horses' – organisation of content and talk for writing, and how they can be harnessed to provide the basis for successful cross-curricular writing.

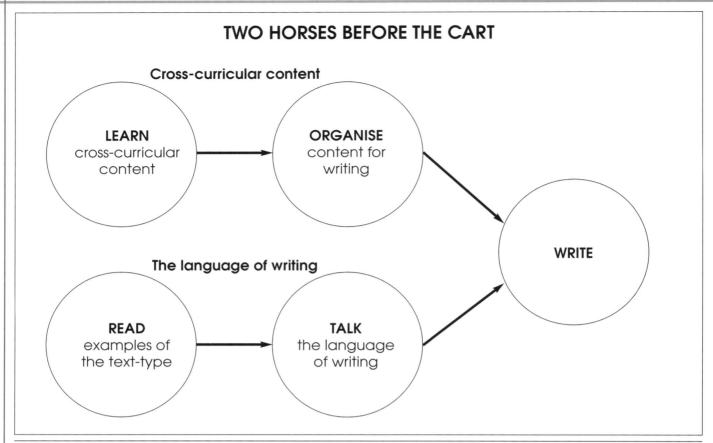

A teaching plan for cross-curricular literacy (simple form)

2 Planning cross-curricular writing

One huge advantage of the National Literacy Strategy and similar national initiatives has been increased attention to non-fiction reading and writing throughout the primary school. In the past, most children in Foundation and Key Stage 1 did only two sorts of writing: 'news' and 'stories'. Over the last decade or so, teachers have begun to cover a much wider range of non-narrative writing skills.

With the introduction of generic non-fiction text-types, the range of children's writing is greatly increased. By the age of seven, most children should now have experience of reading and writing

- **recounts** (see page 41)
- **instructions** (see page 47)
- non-chronological **reports** (see page 53)
- simple **explanation** texts (see page 60).

Although not required by the NLS, children may also have encountered the remaining two text-types: **persuasion** and balanced **discussion**.

The different text-types are characterised by particular sorts of language – recount, for instance, involves the use of the past tense and time connectives, such as *then* and *finally*. They are also characterised by their underlying structures – the way that a particular type of information is organised for writing. Awareness of these structures can become a powerful aid to planning, allowing children to organise their ideas and understanding in the form of notes or pictures before – or, especially in the early stages, instead of – writing.

Skeletons for writing

At Key Stage 2, the National Literacy Strategy has recommended the use of visual planning devices for cross-curricular writing, reflecting the characteristics of each text-type. These planning devices have become known as 'skeletons' (as they are the skeleton frameworks upon which writing can be hung), and a simple skeleton representing each text-type was used on the Key Stage 2 NLS writing fliers (see Appendix 5, Teacher resources).

Since then, extensive work by teachers in Foundation and Key Stage 1 in England and Wales has shown that the use of skeleton planning frameworks is also effective for younger children.

A range of skeletons

Recount – retelling events, in time order

Instruction – how to do something

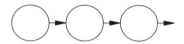

Report – describing what things are like

Explanation – how or why things work or happen

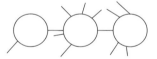

Persuasion – why you should think this

Discussion – reasoned argument

The skeleton frameworks shown here are intended to be representative of each of the non-fiction text-types. As such, they provide a visual 'icon' which reminds children of the structure of the text:

- a **timeline** icon was chosen to represent *recount* because it is a simple, clear indicator of chronological order (using left → right as an indicator of time passing), and is visually easy to remember

- the **simple flowchart** icon for *instructions* demonstrates sequence in the same way, but the circles suggest a number of discrete steps or stages in the process
- in contrast, the **spidergram** icon shows clearly that chronology is not involved in writing *report text*: here the visual display suggests a basic central concept from which radiates information organised into categories
- the **complex flowchart** icon indicates that *explanations* are usually sequential but that there is further contributory detail at each stage: here the sequence involves cause and effect
- the **pronged bullet** icon for *persuasive writing* suggests that the key to organisation is the arranging of arguments into a number of major points, each of which requires elaboration in the form of evidence or further background information
- a **for-and-against grid** suggests that *discussion* text involves the organisation of points + elaboration on both sides of an argument.

Experience suggests that it is best to use the particular skeleton icon as a planning framework when introducing a particular text-type, to help children internalise the underlying structure. However, there are many other ways in which each text-type might be represented, and children should be encouraged to recognise these and choose the one that best suits any individual occasion:

- the sequential, chronological structure of **recount** and **instructions** could be represented by a story-board, a flowchart, a calendar or clockface diagram, or simply a numbered list
- a very simple **report** might be better represented by a labelled picture or diagram; comparative reports often require a grid skeleton
- **explanation** text sometimes requires multiple cause–effect boxes or a cyclical structure (see page 60), or may sometimes be represented by a diagram or sequence of diagrams – in fact, creating graphic representations of the structures underlying individual explanation texts is an excellent way of helping children develop their understanding of cause and effect.

As children become familiar with the idea of skeletons, their repertoire of graphic representations can be gradually enlarged.

How to use skeletons

Skeleton planning provides a link between cross-curricular content and specific teaching of writing skills. Teachers can introduce children to these ways of organising ideas by:

- demonstrating themselves how to use skeletons as simple note-taking devices and aides-memoire throughout the curriculum
- teaching children how to draw the skeletons, and recognise which sorts of ideas and writing are associated with each skeleton
- using skeletons to link knowledge and understanding acquired in a wide range of subject areas with the literacy skills required to record that understanding.

If, for instance, the literacy teaching objective for the week is recount writing, content can be selected from anywhere in the curriculum – perhaps a story from history or a recent activity or outing. The children can help to organise these facts onto a timeline, in the form of brief notes (odd words or phrases), or even pictures. Debbie Billard, a teacher in Rotherham, has coined the term 'memory joggers' for these notes. She explains to the children that memory joggers are not proper sentences – just anything that will jog the class's memory when they come to write.

This timeline can then be used like a carrier bag to bring this cross-curricular content to the literacy lesson. Once children have been taught the relevant language features of recount text, they can use their memory joggers to write. Debbie's suggestion is that they 'turn every memory jogger into a sentence'.

Most of the suggestions for using skeletons at Key Stage 1 have been provided by teachers who, like Debbie Billard, have used them as a planning device for teaching cross-curricular writing to their classes. A selection of case studies is included in the 'Teaching practice' section (page 22), each providing new insights into the teaching process.

Teachers who have used skeleton frameworks with their classes have pointed out a number of advantages:

- making skeleton notes helps children organise what they have learned to aid memorisation of the facts
- many children (especially boys) find it helpful to make this kind of 'big picture' record, so they have an overview of the whole piece of writing before beginning to write (which is, by its nature, a linear sequential process, rather than a holistic one)

- today's children are highly visually literate, and skeleton planning helps them use visual memory skills to aid learning
- as children learn a repertoire of skeletons, they can use them to take notes for a variety of purposes, not just as a precursor to writing
- skeletons allow teachers and children to make clear links between literacy skills and the rest of the curriculum
- planning on a skeleton allows children to organise the content of their writing in advance (including dividing material into sections and paragraphing); it means that when they actually settle down to write, they can concentrate entirely on the language of writing
- making a skeleton with the class, or with a partner, provides an opportunity for highly focused speaking and listening
- using skeletons develops children's thinking skills.

It seems clear from talking to teachers that skeletons have the potential to be more than simple planning devices for writing. Perhaps the most exciting suggestion is that skeleton planning can become a way of developing generic thinking skills – helping children recognise the different ways human beings organise their ideas, depending on the subject matter we are addressing.

This idea is developed further in *Thinking Skills and Eye Q* by Caviglioli, Harris and Tindall (see Appendix 5), in which the authors describe visual planning tools as a means of 'making thinking visible'. In the case studies on pages 22-41, teachers have shown that, through using these visual models, even very young children can grapple with the structures that underlie thought and language.

3 Speaking and listening for cross-curricular writing

The ability to write depends very much upon the ability to speak: until children can articulate their understanding, they are unlikely to be able to turn it into written symbols. They therefore need plenty of opportunities to talk about what they have learned before being expected to write about it. Similarly, the ability to speak depends upon the ability to listen: children learn spoken language through exposure to other, usually more accomplished speakers, such as their teachers.

Any work on cross-curricular writing must therefore take into account the importance of speaking and listening. All the case studies provided in this book (see pages 21–44) lay great emphasis on the provision of opportunities for children to talk about their learning, and to engage in directed discussion with the teacher or other adult to help develop the thinking and language skills necessary for writing about it.

Unfortunately, however, the National Literacy Strategy's *Framework for Teaching*, which has been the driving force behind most schools' practice in the last few years, does not include speaking and listening objectives. Appropriate objectives were defined and listed after the publication of the *Framework* in an excellent document from the QCA (*Teaching Speaking and Listening at Key Stages 1 and 2*, 1999, revised 2003). Again unfortunately, this document has not yet gained widespread recognition in schools. The NLS has also attempted to redress the balance through stressing the importance of activity learning and children's talk in *Developing Early Writing* (2001), and adding speaking and listening objectives to later publications on the internet.

However, the damage has been done. There is a widespread misapprehension that 'the powers that be' no longer place great stress on the importance of speaking and listening in the development of literacy skills. If this misunderstanding is not swiftly cleared up, we could find it having a very deleterious effect on standards of literacy (not to mention children's enjoyment of the curriculum).

There are two points in the process of cross-curricular writing when speaking and listening activities are essential:

- **talk for learning:** when children are internalising ideas and information, talk helps them become familiar with the concepts and vocabulary concerned
- **talk for writing:** before children begin to write, they need opportunities to hear the appropriate forms of language (words, expressions and sentence structures typical of the text-type) and to articulate these forms for themselves.

Talk for learning

In order to understand the content of cross-curricular teaching, young children need – just as they have always needed – plenty of opportunities for talk. These are provided through the sort of good infant practice long recognised as giving valuable opportunities for activity and interaction, such as:

- learning corners and role-play areas, preferably linked to the subject matter concerned, in which children can engage in imaginative play (this is often enhanced by adult involvement in the children's play, expanding vocabulary and ideas)
- outings, excursions, visits and other opportunities to find out about the wider world through experience and talk to a range of adults
- active engagement in learning whenever possible: making, doing, experimenting, learning through play
- plenty of 'props and prompts' for learning – for instance, relevant items to look at, touch and talk about while you are sharing a big book, and opportunities for 'show and tell'
- opportunities to 'experience' factual information, with the teacher's direction, in drama lessons and through specific drama activities like hot-seating
- using puppets to act out what they have learned, and to 'speak through' when explaining something (shy children often find it much easier to talk to a puppet or soft toy than

to the class, and may also be able to respond on a puppet's behalf when they find it difficult to speak up themselves)
- storytelling sessions – listening to the adults telling stories (which can of course be true stories), and having opportunities to tell them themselves
- responding to ideas through music, movement, art and craft.

Without such opportunities for active, motivating learning, young children are unlikely to develop the ideas, concepts, vocabulary and excitement about what they have learned that underpins good writing. With so much attention these days to 'pencil and paper' work it is sometimes tempting to think that this type of practice is a waste of valuable time. In fact, it is the bedrock of literacy.

Experience has shown that certain speaking and listening activities sit particularly comfortably with each of the different text-types, as shown in the boxes. These activities reflect the underlying structures of thought upon which the text-types depend, and thus link to the planning skeletons described in Chapter 3.

Recount content

Before writing recounts, children should be clear on the details and sequence of the story through activities such as:

Retelling Select children to retell short sections of the story to the class. Or ask children in pairs to retell it to each other.

Role-play Ask children in pairs or groups to dramatise significant sections of the story, which they can then re-enact for the class.

Teacher in role Take on the role of a key character in the story yourself, and draw the class with you in re-enacting the story.

Puppetry Let children act out the story with puppets. They can improvise lines as they go, or one child can be narrator, telling the story while the puppets perform.

Freezeframe Ask groups of children to create living tableaux of incidents in the story. Invite participants to step out of each tableau, and comment on what's going on and their part in it.

Instruction content

The best way to familiarise oneself with the content of instructions is actually to carry out the process (or, if that's not possible, watch it), talking it through as you go.

Partnered work Ask the children to carry out the process (or watch it being carried out) in pairs, stopping after each stage to talk through exactly what has been done.

TV demonstration Ask pairs or groups to give a demonstration of the process, describing what they're doing à la Delia Smith or Blue Peter presenters, as if for TV. Others watch and question as necessary.

Running commentary Ask pairs or groups to mime the process, e.g. road safety rules, or act it out with puppets, while others give a running commentary – like a road safety public service broadcast.

Barrier game This is a good way for children to find out whether their instructions are clear enough. Give two children the equipment needed for an activity (e.g. a potato and some Mr Potato Head pieces), place a screen between them so neither can see what the other is doing. One child decides on the activity and carries it out, giving instructions as s/he goes, so the other can mimic it. Remove the barrier and check how successful the instructions were.

Report content

Non-chronological reports involve accurate and clear description. The traditional 'show and tell' is the starting point for this, but you could also use activities like these:

Tell Mr Bear Mr Bear knows absolutely nothing. Ask the children in pairs to work out a clear description of the item/topic in question that will ensure his complete understanding.

Brains Trust When children have found out information on a topic, create a Brains Trust panel so each can give a brief talk to the class on their subject and then answer questions.

TV documentary/newscast Children prepare their own 'open TV presentation' on the subject. This could include commentary, interviews (large felt-tip pens make excellent microphones!) and, where appropriate, mini-dramatisations.

Barrier game With two children, give one child a simple picture or artefact related to the topic and place a screen between the two so the other child can't see it. The first child must describe the item so that the second can draw it, or pick out a duplicate from a given selection. (When using barrier games to practise description, illustrated wrapping paper – e.g. paper with lots of pictures of cats – can be useful. Give the first child a cut-out of one cat, and the second a complete sheet to spot the appropriate cat.)

Another aspect of non-chronological report writing is the development of categorisation skills:

Sorting activities Most infant classrooms have games or activities requiring children to sort items into groups, e.g. model animals, coloured shapes, pictures of activities. Provide items of this sort related to cross-curricular work, and ask children in pairs to sort them into groups, then explain the reasons behind their choices.

In the hoop Lay a number of hoops on the ground to represent different categories within your current project (e.g. fruit, dairy products, meat, vegetables for a Food project). Ask each child to complete a sentence (e.g. 'A . . . is a kind of . . . .') and go to stand in the correct hoop.

The corner game Choose four categories related to your topic, and make signs to put in the four corners of the hall to indicate the categories. On slips of paper write words or phrases, or draw pictures, which fit into one or other of the categories. Children take a slip and read it, then run around the hall till a given signal, such as a whistle, when they must rush to the appropriate corner. Each child (or selected children) then explains their presence in their particular corner: 'My paper says . . . . I came to the . . . corner because . . . .'

Explanation content

The best way to familiarise children with scientific concepts such as cause and effect is through involving them in meaningful activities, followed by discussion,

as demonstrated in the 'Scooters' section of the NLS Developing Early Writing video (see Appendix 5, Teacher resources). Other preliminary activities could involve:

Physical theatre Think up a way to dramatise the process, changing children into caterpillars that turn into butterflies, bones/muscles in an arm, seeds that grow, etc. Pairs or groups mime the process, while others give a commentary.

Teacher (or puppet) in role You (or the puppet) act the part of an earnest but very dim seeker after knowledge, requiring the clearest of clear explanations.

Another way of helping children internalise their understanding of cross-curricular content is to help them arrange the information on a skeleton planning framework, in the form of memory joggers (words, phrases, pictures). This can be a whole-class activity: the case studies on pages 22–41 contain many ingenious suggestions for involving children in creating class skeleton notes. Or, once children are familiar with skeleton planning, pairs of children can be asked to make their own timelines, spidergrams, etc. organising the content they have learned elsewhere in the curriculum. Skeletons thus provide a means of planning which also doubles as a useful opportunity for focused talk.

Talk for writing

Once children have grasped the content they are to write about, they need help in acquiring appropriate language structures to express it. As is shown on pages 41, 47, 53 and 60, each of the four text-types covered in Key Stage 1 is characterised by certain language features.

It is not particularly helpful for young children to go into grammatical details of these language features (although by Year 2 certain grammatical terms, such as *verb* and *noun*, may be helpful to allow generalisations, e.g. 'When you're writing about the past, a lot of verbs end in –ed'; see Appendix 3). Much more important is a growing familiarity with the types of words, phrases and sentence structures associated with each text-type.

There are many ways we can build up this familiarity:

● through **reading examples of the text-type**, talking about how authors express their ideas, and collecting examples of the sorts of language they use, e.g.

- the past tense and time connectives in recount
- imperative ('bossy') verbs in instructions
- the present tense and the use of examples in report
- causal language structures in explanation.
- through **sentence-level activities** to help children recognise grammatical patterns underlying many of these language features, e.g.
  - games in which verbs must be changed into the past tense
  - class collections of words and phrases (e.g. posters for time connectives or cause-and-effect words; a bank of useful adjectives – *Words for big*, *Words for little*, etc.).
- through **focused speaking and listening activities** in which children create sentences of their own, featuring the appropriate language features (see the box, 'Using Speaking Frames').

Using 'speaking frames'

Listen → Imitate → Innovate → Invent

This four-stage sequence sums up how children acquire new forms of language from their earliest days. It can be used as a model for ensuring they are familiar with language forms and structures characteristic of the written texts we want them to produce.

- **Listen** Children hear examples from exemplar texts read aloud, e.g. clear, concise introductory sentences: '*My name is Jessica Martin and I am six years old. I live in Manchester with my mum and my little brother Baz...*'

- **Imitate** Children familiarise themselves with the language patterns as they read the exemplar text aloud themselves.

- **Innovate** Children think of information related to themselves which could fit into a 'speaking frame' based on the examples:

  '*My name is ... and I am ... years old. I live in ... with ....*'

- **Invent** Once familiar with a construction, children should be able to use it – and adapt it – in various ways in their own speech and writing.

Often we expect children to go straight to the 'inventing' stage with little or no

---

opportunity to internalise language structures through the experiences of the earlier stages. It is therefore worth looking for ways to integrate the **Listen → Imitate → Innovate → Invent** sequence into our teaching to familiarise children with written language patterns (including sentence constructions), and to allow them the experience of producing, from their own mouths, more sophisticated language than they would usually use.

The innovation stage, using a 'speaking frame', should be a regular part of shared work. More able children should try 'filling in' the speaking frame first, so that the less able have the opportunity to hear it several times before it comes to their turn. After half a dozen or so children have had a go, so that everyone is comfortable with the construction, everyone can be asked to 'fill in' the speaking frame for their partner. (More able children could be given the task of conveying the same information in different words.)

Speaking frames can be devised for any sort of language use, including practising the use of connectives, voicing opinions, and rehearsing sentence structures for comparison, contrast, cause and effect, etc.

Paired work

The great problem in providing opportunities for structured talk is that there are thirty or so children in a class needing to talk and only one teacher available to listen. The NLS's solution to this is paired talk. You allocate each child a 'talking partner', someone with whom they can be trusted to work well. Whenever the opportunity arises you can say: 'Turn to your partner. You have 30 seconds [or two minutes, or whatever] to discuss...' Selected pairs can then retell their deliberations to the class.

Teachers who have used this system effectively stress the importance of training and careful organisation.

- Most children need considerable training to do it well. They can be trained during Guided Writing time, which is often more appropriately Guided Talk. One child works as the teacher's partner to model the appropriate behaviour, then the group splits into pairs to try it. There should also be opportunities for the group to discuss the point of the exercise, and good and bad points of procedure.

- Where there is a teaching assistant in the class, the teacher and assistant can model a paired discussion before asking the children to try it.
- Snippets of NLS training videos can also be useful for showing the class how the system works. The short 'Taking a closer look' section at the end of 'Scooters' on the *Developing Early Writing* video is a good example.
- Children should be suitably paired. Most teachers find ability pairings work best, but obviously this varies depending on the children. Pairs should be reviewed frequently to check that the children are still happy working together.
- Pupils should automatically sit next to their partner for literacy – it helps to have marks on the floor (e.g. carpet squares) in the literacy corner.
- It also helps to have posters on the wall as reminders of routines.

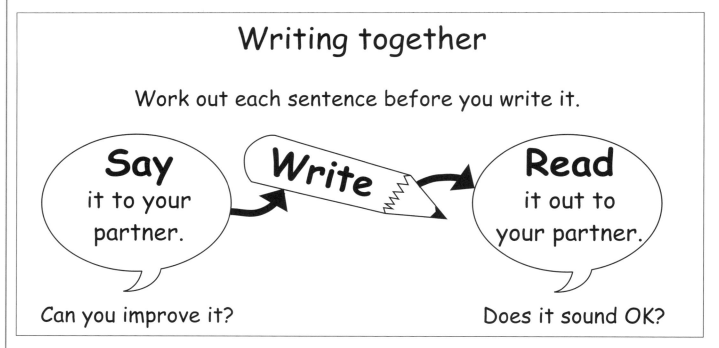

Writing together

Work out each sentence before you write it.

Say it to your partner.

Can you improve it?

Write

Read it out to your partner.

Does it sound OK?

Activities of this kind may seem time consuming but, in the long run, children's literacy development is likely to be accelerated by increased opportunities for structured, directed speaking and listening.

There is one final occasion on which 'talk for writing' is important at Foundation and Key Stage 1, that is, at the very moment that children are actually engaged in writing. Oral rehearsal of each sentence (or in longer sentences, each clause) helps children

- think of the idea they are expressing as a whole
- check that what they are about to write makes sense
- remember what they are writing as they tussle with the problems of transcription
- anticipate how the writing will sound.

The routine below, devised by a teacher in Bolton, sums up the stages in composition admirably. Teachers can demonstrate this procedure themselves in Shared Writing, and encourage children to use it during independent work.

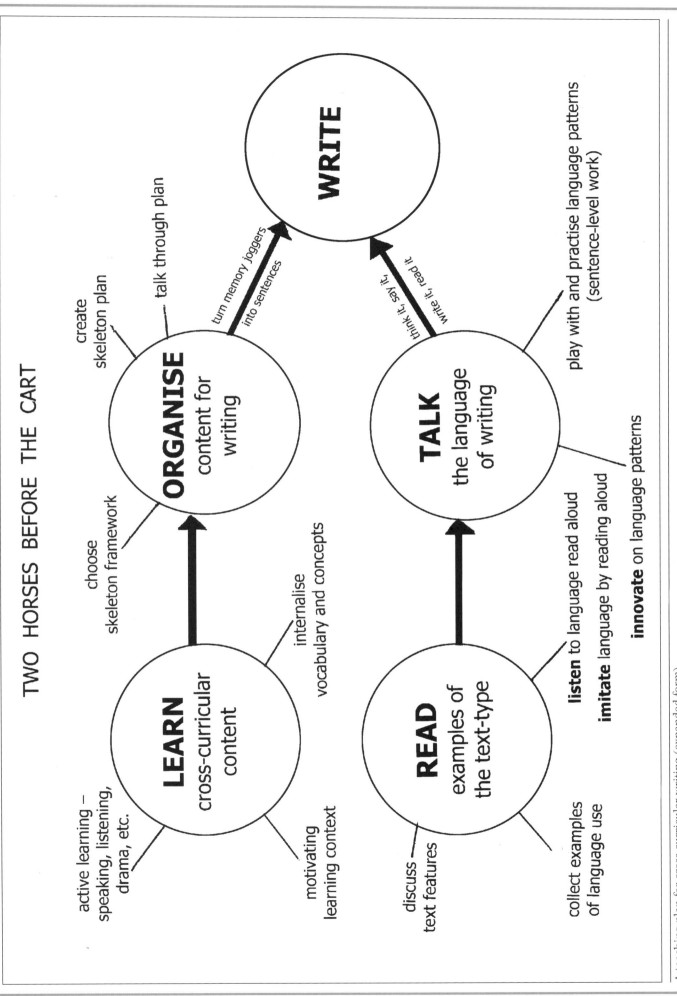

TWO HORSES BEFORE THE CART

WRITE

ORGANISE content for writing

- create skeleton plan
- talk through plan
- choose skeleton framework

turn memory joggers into sentences

LEARN cross-curricular content

- active learning – speaking, listening, drama, etc.
- internalise vocabulary and concepts
- motivating learning context

TALK the language of writing

- play with and practise language patterns (sentence-level work)
- **innovate** on language patterns
- **imitate** language by reading aloud
- **listen** to language read aloud

think it, say it, write it, read it

READ examples of the text-type

- discuss text features
- collect examples of language use

A teaching plan for cross-curricular writing (expanded form)

Teaching practice
4 Recount Writing case studies

From the very earliest stages, we can use pictures or simple words on timelines to help children recognise time order, and use it to recall specific events. A timeline can provide a useful focus for highly directed speaking and listening activities.

1. Nursery: Our day at school

Maggie Greenhalgh, headteacher of The Abbey School, Glastonbury, made a timeline with seven nursery children, all four years old. She talked with the children about what they do at school, then asked them to choose an aspect of the day to draw. Maggie pinned up a timeline along the wall and the children chose the order to put the pictures along it. She reported that, all in all, their ability to sequence their daily activities was extremely good, and the exercise was a 'useful way to develop thinking skills, as well as beginning the continuum of teaching for recount writing'.

Having introduced the idea, Maggie could see many other ways of using timelines with this age group, to help improve children's appreciation of chronological order in preparation for writing when they were older. She intended to make two timelines of the trip the class would be going on in a week's time:

- one before, to use as a focus for talking about the trip in advance, and to help children think about it and give them a framework of events to expect
- one after, to help them recall and record what happened.

2. Year 1: The wedding

It is relatively easy these days to record actual events as they happen, using a digital camera. Photographs can be used to create a timeline, and to provide a motivating focus for children's talk before writing.

Tara Chappell and Anne Hulley of Wybourn Primary School, Sheffield, used photographs as part of an RE project about 'Weddings', in which Year 1 children created a wedding planner portfolio for a member of staff about to be married. After a number of other activities involving writing in a variety of non-fiction genres, the class staged their own wedding with children taking the parts of the bride, groom, vicar, guests and so on. The ceremony was videoed and

Playing in the computer room with Sadie.

Writing my name.

Playing with the popoids.

Playtime

Picture timeline of a school day, by nursery children at The Abbey School, Glastonbury. In the earliest stages, timelines can help to

photographed (just like a real wedding), and these records provided a visual record of the event when the class came to write about it.

Watching the ceremony on video provided many opportunities for directed talk about their wedding, after which the pupils were well equipped to organise a sequence of photographs to retell the events in chronological order. The teachers used these for Shared Writing, over a number of short sessions. These teaching sessions were based on the structure provided in the NLS book *Developing Early Writing* (2001). Each provided an opportunity to emphasise one aspect of recount writing, as well as revision of other word- and sentence-level teaching.

In session 1, the teacher gave a demonstration of how to convey the information in the picture as two sentences, both in the past tense:

> Now, what happened in this photo? Who's waiting at the ceremony? The groom is waiting. So, how shall I say that? – it's not happening now. I need to say *waited*. *The groom waited at the end of the aisle.* Next I want to say something about what the groom looked like. Now, I need to remember to start my sentence with a capital letter. *He was wearing a very smart black suit with a flower in his button hole.* I wonder, how do I write *flower*? I'll say it slowly and stretch it out. How many sounds are there? *f-l-ow-er* – four. There!

The children then wrote their own sentences to describe what was happening in the picture. In session 2, the class decided on another sentence for the teacher to scribe: *The bride and bridesmaids came down the aisle*:

> Now I want to add something more to that sentence, because the bride came after the groom. Look at our connectives board we made – *after that, next, in a while, suddenly, all of a sudden, then, straight after that*.... Which connective can we start our new sentence with? We want to say something about the bride appearing after the groom, to use one of our time connectives. Turn to your partners and compose the sentence starting with a time connective.... I'm going to use Nicola's idea because I like the way she used *in a while* from our time connectives board, and the past tense word *walked*.

Children in pairs then looked at the next picture in the sequence (the ceremony) and composed a sentence about it, beginning with a time connective. They wrote this on their individual whiteboards. For independent work, they wrote about the next picture in the sequence. In the third session, the recount was completed, using the same technique.

3. Year 2: Grace Darling

Debbie Billard at East Dene School in Rotherham introduced the use of timeline skeletons to her Year 2 class, as part of their project on the seaside. To first familiarise them with the concept, she read them a recount about heroism at sea – the story of Tom Bowker (see Appendix 4). Although this was a demanding passage for Year 2, the children liked the story, and it inspired plenty of discussion – talking about the unusual words and asking 'why' questions about what happened.

e concept of left–right sequencing.

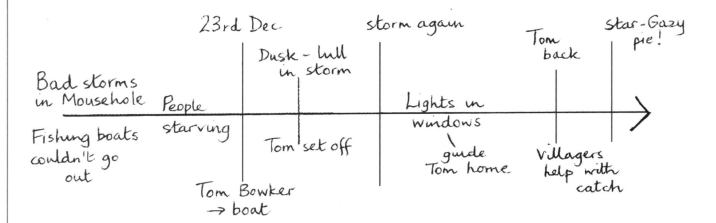

She then showed how to put the main events on to a timeline (above).

The children took to the idea of this visual representation very easily, which Debbie felt reflected a high level of visual literacy, due to their familiarity with TV and computers: 'Today's children are very comfortable with this type of visual display, and I think we should make use of that in developing literacy skills.'

Meanwhile, the class was involved in a history topic on Grace Darling. This featured another story of heroism at sea, which Debbie told to the children, reinforcing their understanding by the use of drama (freezeframing), role-play (hot-seating) and artwork. Once the children were familiar with the events, they were enthusiastic about helping to put them on a timeline. Debbie demonstrated how to reduce the key details of the story to 'memory joggers' (words, phrases or little pictures – whatever would best help them remember the details when they came to write). She preferred the term 'memory joggers' because it was more meaningful to them than the conventional term 'notes'.

She then gave the class a free choice of how to make their own timeline models of the Grace Darling story. Some did it completely in pictures, some used a mixture of pictures and labels. 'I watched one boy carefully draw a series of circles across a strip of paper, number them, then draw a captioned picture in each. I think it's really important that children should make their own decisions about how to present information – it gives them confidence and ownership of the content. Even the less able children could record their understanding in this way, and then talk through the story with a partner.'

Next she showed how to plan an introduction to set the scene for readers by answering some key questions:

- Who is the story about?
- What did she do?
- Where did it happen?
- When did it happen?

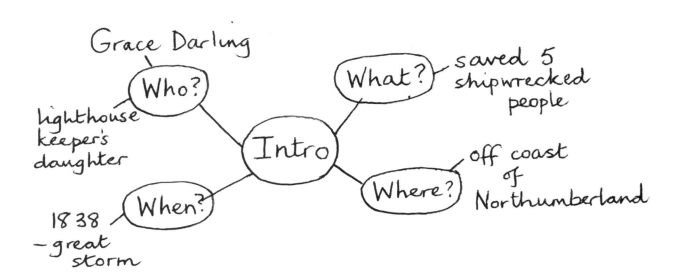

The class discussed how the memory joggers on the skeleton could be turned into sentences for writing, then used their timelines to write their own versions of the story. Debbie reported that the results were 'amazing': 'A supply teacher who knows the class well said, "I can't believe the standard of the writing." I think it's because they had the timeline there in front of them, so they didn't have to worry about what to write, they could just concentrate on how to write it. Even the less able children, who found chronology difficult, just kept referring back to their timelines – I'm sure visual models like this will help develop their memory skills. As for the more able, it freed them up to think about vocabulary and expression – they used some lovely words and phrases, better connectives and more varied sentence openings. The standard improved for every child.'

More ideas

The following list has been compiled from ideas from teachers all over the country who have used timelines with their classes:

- A timeline skeleton does not have to be carefully designed and neatly made. A quick timeline can be created on the board to remind children of any sequence of events being discussed. This helps reinforce the idea of chronology.
- It isn't important (especially at Key Stage 1) to be particularly exact about spacing on the timeline to show the passage of time – a small space for a short time and a larger space for a longer time is quite adequate. However, by Year 2, if you are recording, say, the events of a particular week, or a child's life story, it may be helpful to divide the timeline into roughly equal sections to illustrate days or years.
- To ensure children grasp the concept of chronology, timelines should go in a continuous line from left to right. For class timelines, you therefore need a long strip of paper – old wallpaper or decorator's lining paper is good – or many educational suppliers do rolls of newsprint or frieze paper.
- Children's pictures or notes can be stuck along the timeline with Blu-tack, or children can write or draw on Post-it notes – most stationers now stock lots of shapes, colours and sizes.

Reception children at Sacred Heart Catholic Primary School, Southend-on-Sea, using photographs to make a timeline of their day at school.

- A Velcro strip attached along a wall (or even along the top of a storage unit) can be used for any sequencing activity. Pictures or notes on pieces of card with Velcro dots can then be stuck along it – children love Velcro!
- Children can hold their pictures or notes and stand in order to create a human timeline. Or cards can be pegged along a washing line.
- For children's own timelines, sugar paper or A3 white paper can be cut into strips (lengthwise) and sellotaped together. This means they can add more if their timeline grows longer than they expect!
- Other useful materials are fax rolls, adding machine rolls and wallpaper friezes (but the self-adhesive type don't work, because you can't write on them).

See also speaking and listening activities for 'Recount text', page 17.

Mr Richardson –
guide showed us
- saddlestone
- quernstone

sketched
mill building

visited millpond –
water to drive mill

saw flour bags
from old days

There is great potential for using computers to create skeleton notes, although the shape of the screen means their application with timelines and flowcharts is limited. However, as this example from East Dene School shows, a limited number of pictures displayed across a wide screen (interactive whiteboard) can be very effective

5 Report Writing case studies

1. Year 1: Healthy and unhealthy foods

Caroline Richardson, at East Dene School in Rotherham, used the spidergram skeleton with her Year 1 class as part of their topic work on 'Health'. Since she has an interactive whiteboard in her classroom, she was able to use this to illustrate how ideas can be organised into categories.

As part of an investigation of healthy and unhealthy food, the children drew pictures of a variety of foods, which were scanned and displayed on the whiteboard. Caroline created two circles, one labelled 'Healthy foods', and the other 'Unhealthy foods', and the children then used a pointer to move the pictures so that they were gathered around the appropriate circle.

It is easy to move pictures and words about on the whiteboard screen, so Caroline then helped the class devise subcategories – 'fruit' and 'vegetables' for Healthy foods, and 'sugary foods' and 'fatty foods' for Unhealthy foods, and created 'arms' on the spidergram for each. The children then reorganised the pictures into these subcategories. They now had a clear visual representation of their discussions about food – a representation of which they had ownership, since it was their own pictures and they had done all the physical manipulation of the images themselves.

Caroline used the whiteboard model as the basis of a variety of writing tasks, depending on the children's ability, and noted improvements in their writing: 'The pupils have been eager to work in this way and enjoy the visual aspects of the work produced. Using the new technology alongside the skeletons has provided a good working example of the integration of ICT within literacy work, with successful results.'

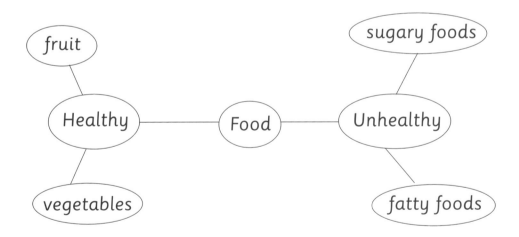

2. Year 2: How we are different

Cecilia Tallon of Sacred Heart Catholic Primary School in Southend-on-Sea developed a large-scale version of the report skeleton to introduce categorisation skills in a Year 2 class. As part of their topic work on 'How we are different', the children each came up with one sentence about 'something I like'. These were printed out in large type, so that each child could hold the sentence s/he had composed.

Hoops were laid out on the floor and the children used a 'Get up and go' sorting activity to group the sentences. To start with, children stood in the hoop they thought most appropriate, but could move to another if, after discussion, they changed their minds. When this got too busy, they changed to placing the sentence strips in the hoops instead. Categories began to emerge, to which they gave broad titles like 'Food', 'Clothes'

'Hobbies'. These could subsequently be used label the appropriate hoop.

In Shared Writing, the teacher demonstrated how to write an introductory paragraph, pointing out that people's tastes are different, and summarising the categories to be explored. She then scribed as children from the 'Food' hoop used their sentences to create a paragraph on food preferences. Groups of children, with one acting as a scribe, were then able to write up the facts from the other categories, and their work was gathered together in a class book. 'We also put the hoops on the wall as part of the display,' said Cecilia, 'because the visual impact really helped with the idea of categorisation. I think the opportunity for children to stand in the hoops was useful too – it gave a concrete, physical aspect to an abstract process. The children could see that, if necessary, they could move from hoop to hoop as they organised and reorganised their thoughts.'

Large-scale activities, like Cecilia Tallon's hoop spidergram, help make the process of organising their ideas more meaningful for children.

3. Year 2: Seaside holidays

Continuing her topic on the sea (see page 23), Debbie Billard, of East Dene School in Rotherham, used the spidergram report skeleton to help children plan a piece of writing on 'Seaside holidays'. She used the BOSsing technique described in 'More ideas' (p. 30).

To begin with, the class brainstormed ideas about holidays at the seaside, which Debbie noted on the board. The children then discussed how these ideas could be organised into groups, and chose the headings: Things we do/see/eat at the seaside. Debbie used coloured crayons to indicate the category for each memory jogger, then drew a spidergram diagram and began to fit the information into it.

The more able children understood the principle very quickly and were able to go off and make their own spidergrams, using the brainstorm notes. The fact that Debbie had suggested turning each arm of the skeleton into a seaside bucket may have helped make the task more attractive! She completed the spidergram on the board with the rest of the class, after which they made their own 'bucket' versions.

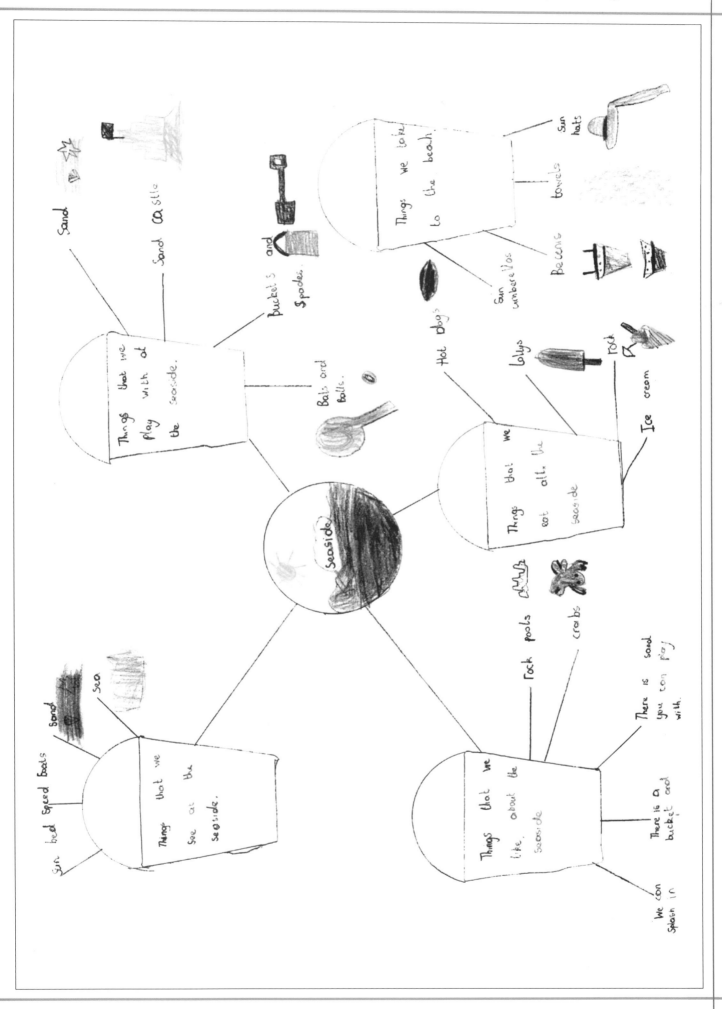

The less able children used these notes to write about 'Holidays now'. In shared work, Debbie reminded them how to turn each of the memory joggers on the class spidergram into a sentence and write it. They then continued this process in pairs – making up each sentence orally, then writing it. Debbie found the oral rehearsal particularly successful: 'They even wanted to do their writing as afternoon work – and still got great results!'

Meanwhile, Debbie worked with the more able group to research information about seaside holidays in the past, which created another bucket of memory joggers. This more able group then used the paired system to write about 'Seaside holidays, now and in the past'. This group could see clearly how the spidergram skeleton organised the information into separate chunks, so they were able to follow a further instruction when writing up the notes: 'Leave a line after each bucket.' Their writing then fell neatly into paragraphs.

More ideas

The following list has been compiled from ideas from teachers all over the country who have used spidergrams with their classes.

- The steps involved in making a spidergram are summarised in the acronym **BOS**:
  - **B**RAINSTORM children's knowledge and ideas, noting them in any order
  - **O**RGANISE the ideas into categories, to create a spidergram. Add more ideas as it develops
  - **S**pidergram provides the content for report text with a heading and subheadings (or just organised into paragraphs).
- During the brainstorming session, children can be asked to jot memory joggers on to Post-it notes. When you are ready to organise their ideas into categories, the Post-it notes can be repositioned in the appropriate place.
- Alternatively, memory joggers can be written on card and a dab of Blu-tack placed on the back. These can then be moved around in the same way.

Hoops can also be used to create a wall display showing how ideas may be arranged into categories

- The computer program *Kidspiration* is designed for 'mapping' spidergrams and other diagrams of this type (see Appendix 5).
- Children can create human spidergrams by holding a card and standing in a designated area, such as a hoop (as in Case study 2 above), which represents their 'category'.
- For a comparative report (e.g. 'Looking after a pet'), it is often helpful to brainstorm and organise information for one type of pet, then use the chosen categories to create a grid, covering several different pets, e.g.:

	dog	cat	gerbil
food			
exercise			
bed			

- For older children, spidergram notes are often much more effective than traditional notes for prepared talks. A simple (and brief) memory jogger acts as a stimulus to the child to talk about what s/he knows, while traditional notes tend to trap the speaker into attempting to follow a sequential pattern which is not easily memorised.

See also the speaking and listening activities for 'Report text', page 17.

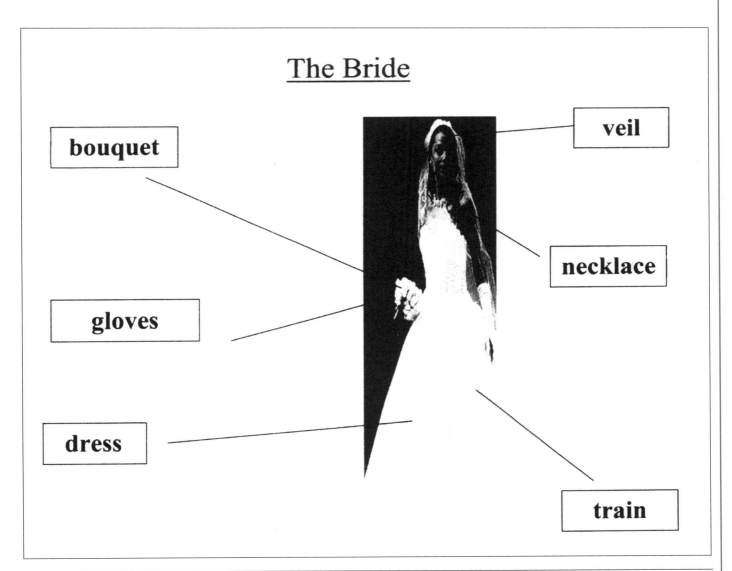

This display from Year 1's 'Wedding' project at Wybourn Primary School, Sheffield, demonstrates how photographs can be used to create spidergram notes

6 Instruction Writing case studies

Most instructions are a series of sequenced steps, which can be shown on a *flowchart* skeleton. Depending on the age and ability of the children they can use pictures, key words or a mixture of both for this skeleton planning. Making a flowchart helps them sort out the stages in the process and the sequence of events, without the added cognitive burden involved in writing.

1. Year 2: Making honey biscuits

Hayley Williams at Comin Infants School in Aberdare, South Wales, used a flowchart to record the steps in 'making honey biscuits' with her Year 2 class. Her class had done instructional writing before, so they had had plenty of practice of the appropriate language features. She was therefore interested in using a mixture of skeleton planning and focused talk to improve their understanding of the structure of instruction text.

She first modelled how to make a flowchart for making toast, showing the class how to draw the circles and arrows, and how to write notes, not sentences. (They were thrilled to know this was a chance to write without capitals and full stops!) She then demonstrated how to use the finished flowchart to retell the whole process.

Then, after they had made their honey biscuits, the children made their own flowcharts, with pictures and words for each step. They worked collaboratively, talking through the process, and making decisions about what to include in each step. Hayley reported that this activity was very useful for reinforcing the vocabulary and helping them remember what was involved.

When the children's flowcharts were complete, she revised the layout and language features of instruction text, using this page from *The Instruction Book* (one of the Skeleton Poster Books, see Appendix 5).

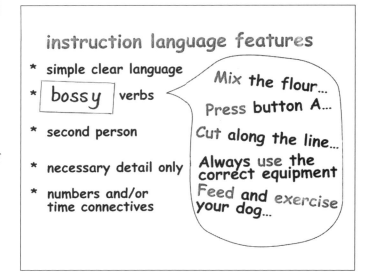

She also taught a routine for collaborative writing which would encourage oral rehearsal before they wrote (see page 20), so that they really thought through each sentence.

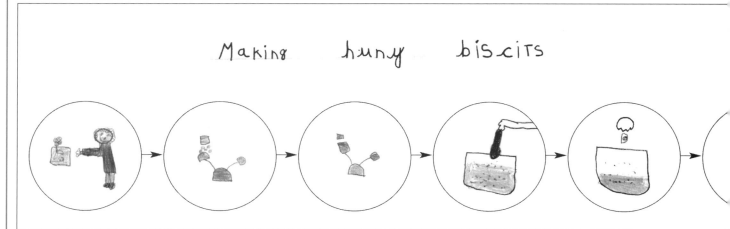

A recipe flowchart by a reception child from Comin Infants School

The children needed a fair amount of time to write up their recipes in this way, but Hayley was convinced that it was worth it: 'Previously the children had mixed things up or got steps in the wrong order but, with the flowchart to refer to, this didn't happen. They could concentrate on the techniques of writing – putting in the detail, the connectives and so on. It meant they needed very little guidance – the teaching assistant and I moved around chatting to various pairs, but they were able to use their partners to practise sentences. The results were excellent. We couldn't believe how straightforward it was to teach writing in this way. Now we've seen it, it seems so obvious, we can't think why we didn't do it before!'

Nasir
Hoeny Biscits.
What you need.
ot oten.   Cooking tray
Way ing Scale.   Suger.
Flower.   Hoeny.
cinnamon.   or egg.
            What you do.
1. Put the oven on t 175°C.
2. Wash yo hands.
3. Way the buter and suger and you must have 120g echa
4. beat the buter and suger until its crethe.
5. add a large tablespoon of Honey.
6. separate the egg york
7. stire the mixtra together.
8. put a teaspoon of cinnamon.
9. role it until its able Looks Like ad
10. role it until its a bode.
11. put it in a cooking tryp until 12-15 mins
Then enjoy
                            Year 2

2. Reception: Making honey biscuits

Mette Cartwright, also in Comin Infants, tried the activity with Reception children, using pictures rather than notes. She started by telling them about flowcharts and drew one to show how they work. The next day they made the biscuits, and gathered with Mette to decide how they could draw their flowcharts. She started it off, then the children went away and each did their own. When they had finished, they took it in turns to retell the recipe from the pictures.

Mette reported: 'It was a delight to watch them, and it really focused them on the steps and the sequence! I'll be getting this class in Year 1, and I can already see the next step – accompanying the pictures with a few labels and phrases... it should be a brilliant foundation for when they eventually write the whole recipe.'

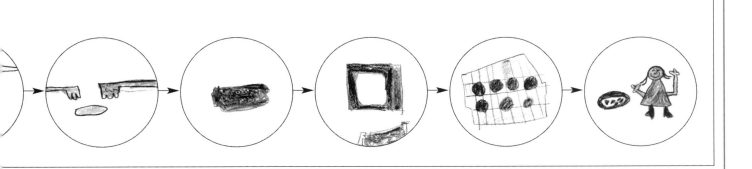

3. Year 2: How to cross the road

Kaye Pilcher of Roskear Primary School in Cambourne, Cornwall, used an instruction skeleton, along with role-play, as part of a school project on 'Safety'. The class began with a discussion about road safety in general, and then focused particularly on how to cross a road. Kaye noted the points children made on Post-it notes. Many of them related to safe places to cross, e.g. 'lollipop lady', 'no parked cars', 'no corners'. Others related to behaviour at the roadside or when crossing the road.

She then modelled how to select and order the Post-it notes to make an instruction skeleton for crossing at a zebra, which she wrote up on the board:

Step Two: Wait on the kerb until the cars have stopped and the road is clear'). Each trio of children then used their own skeleton notes to practise a similar road safety ad, to perform to the class.

Later, the class read and discussed the language and layout of samples of written instruction text. They used a mixture of Shared, Guided and Independent Writing to create their own illustrated information sheet on 'How to cross the road safely'.

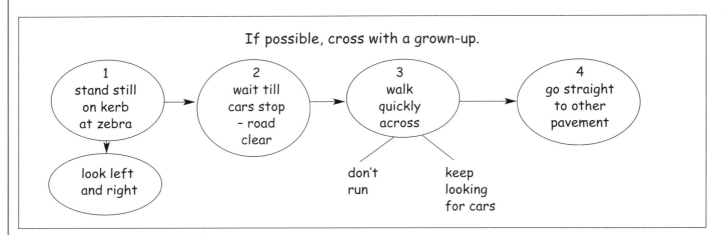

Next she asked children, in threes, to make similar skeleton plans for crossing the road:

- at a pelican crossing
- at the lollipop man or lady
- at a stretch of road with no parked cars or corners.

She worked with a guided group of six on the skeleton for the last scenario, as it was the most difficult.

Next Kaye modelled how to use her zebra skeleton plan as an aide memoire for a role-play activity. Two children acted out a road safety 'TV advert', based on the skeleton, while Kaye spoke the instructions. She modelled how to convert the memory joggers on the skeleton script into spoken sentences (e.g. 'This is how to cross the road at a zebra crossing. Step One: Stand very still on the kerb at the zebra crossing and look left and right.

More ideas

- There are a number of elements in a piece of instruction writing, not just the sequence of instructions. The poster on the opposite page (taken from *The Instruction Book*) provides a visual prompt.
- Instruction skeletons are best drawn from left to right, thus using organisation to indicate time sequence and reinforcing left ➜ right orientation. As for timelines, steps can be drawn horizontally across strips of paper (see page 26), or drawn on card and pegged on a washing line, held by children, or stuck along a Velcro strip.
- Sequences of classroom instructions can also be presented in this way – for example, the 'Writing together' poster on page 20.

instruction organisation

Title:
what's to be
achieved

Maybe...
labelled
diagram(s)

What you need
• - - - - - - - - - -
• - - - - - - - - - -
• - - - - - - - - - -
• - - - - - - - - - -

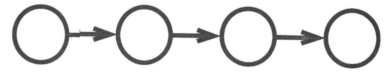

What to do, one step at a time

Children at Sacred Heart Catholic Primary School in Southend-on-Sea created 'human instructions', using hoops to symbolise the steps in the process. The child in the hoop acted out that step.

How to make gingerbread men

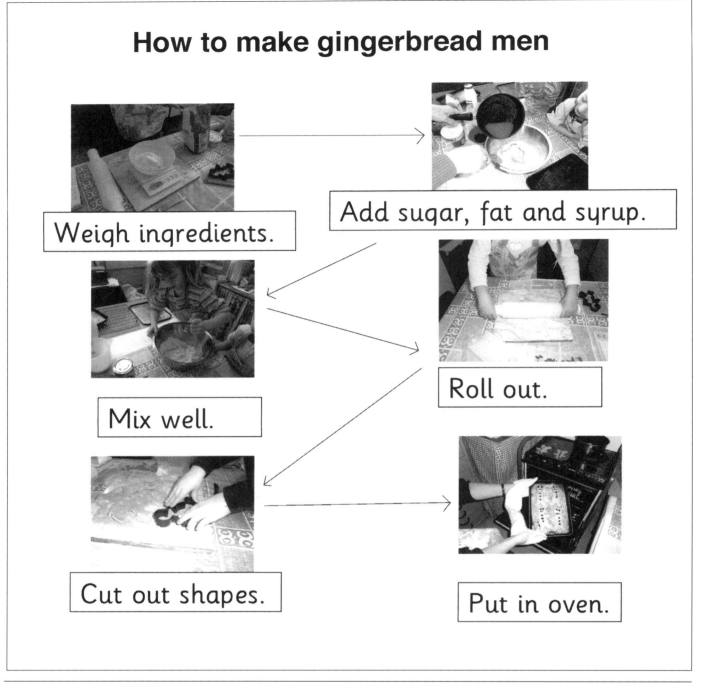

Weigh ingredients.

Add sugar, fat and syrup.

Mix well.

Roll out.

Cut out shapes.

Put in oven.

Once children are familiar with flowcharts, the technique can be used in ICT, with illustrations provided by digital camera, as in this example by Debbie Billard of East Dene Primary School, Rotherham.

7 Explanation Writing case studies

The National Literacy Strategy requires teachers in England to cover recount, report and instruction writing during Key Stage 1. Explanation writing – the more difficult task of explaining how or why something happens – is not covered in any detail until Key Stage 2, but the foundations are established earlier. By the end of Year 2, children should have experience of

- drawing and reading flowcharts depicting sequences of cause and effect
- composing cause and effect sentences, using connectives such as *because*, *so* and *if*.

Both of these objectives can be covered in cross-curricular work on science, geography or history themes.

1. Year 2: How babies grow

Rachel Kitchen, Year 2 teacher at Yew Tree Primary School in Dukinfield, Tameside, tried using a flowchart as part of her project on Food and Growth. She began with shared reading of the big book *How Babies Grow* by Neate and Henry,

which stimulated a great deal of discussion about babies in the children's own families. Many children had younger siblings and their first-hand knowledge meant they were very interested in the topic.

Rachel produced enlarged copies of the pictures provided in Appendix 4, demonstrating child development from birth to two years, and the children helped organise them in order on the board and draw arrows to create a growth flowchart. They then discussed what they knew about each stage, and drew lines outwards from the pictures to write key words about aspects of development. Rachel noted that the children had no trouble with the concept of 'key words' in this context: 'When I asked "Why aren't I writing this in sentences?" they gave two reasons: first, there wouldn't be enough room; second, it wouldn't be as easy to read and get the information quickly.'

It led her to question the traditional method of teaching how to take notes: 'Teachers tend to jump straight into showing how to take notes from books, the way we were taught to do it ourselves – "We're going to read this page and then we'll identify the key words". I think that for most children the whole thing must seem pointless and

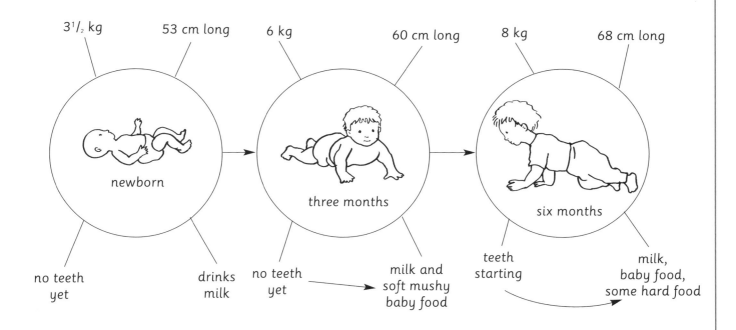

irrelevant, which is probably why they find it so hard. But recording what you've learned on a skeleton is fun and it's meaningful – the memory jogger words and phrases just come naturally.'

After this demonstration of how to make the flowchart, the pupils tried making them for themselves, using photocopied versions of the same pictures. They worked in pairs, talking through the facts to make their notes. Rachel noted that 'They loved the activity and I felt they had learned a lot more from it than just reading and discussing information from a book.'

The following day they revisited the class flowchart and used it to explore the language of cause and effect. She asked the children to create some sentences about the baby that would answer the question 'Why?' After making up lots of 'Why' questions, the children composed sentences to answer them. They did this orally, and used a variety of connectives, for instance:

'The baby can eat solid food now **because** it has got teeth.'
'The baby has grown stronger now **so** it can stand up.'
'**When** the baby drinks milk it grows bigger **and** its teeth start to grow.'

Rachel used some of these ideas in a piece of Shared Writing, converting the flowchart notes into the class's own passage about how babies grow. The children helped turn each of the key facts on the flowchart into a sentence, and the layout of the flowchart meant the facts organised themselves naturally into paragraphs.

Rachel felt that skeletons were an aid to good teaching: 'I really like the idea of using diagrams like this as an aid to writing. They help single out the different elements involved in teaching

something. You can concentrate first on children's understanding, then on organising and recording the key facts, then on turning what they've learned into sentences.'

2. Year 2: Ourselves

Peter Scott of Totley Primary School in Sheffield used explanation skeletons as part of a topic on 'Health and growth'. He introduced children to various types of explanation, starting with the straightforward cause-and-effect model. After an experiment to find out how high the children could jump, the class created graphs of their efforts which tended to follow this pattern:

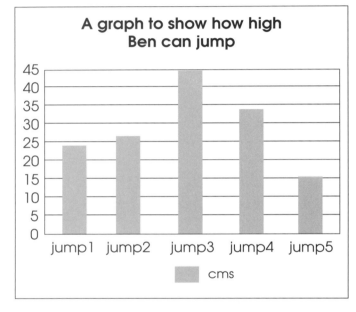

They then discussed the possible reasons for the pattern, and represented them as the linear cause-and-effect flowchart shown below.

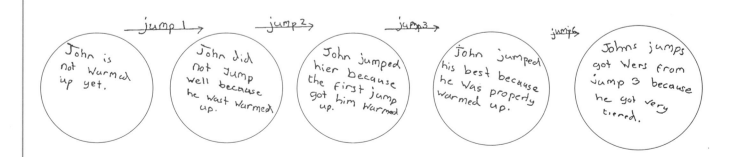

A general discussion on aspects of healthy
living resulted in this multiple-cause flowchart:

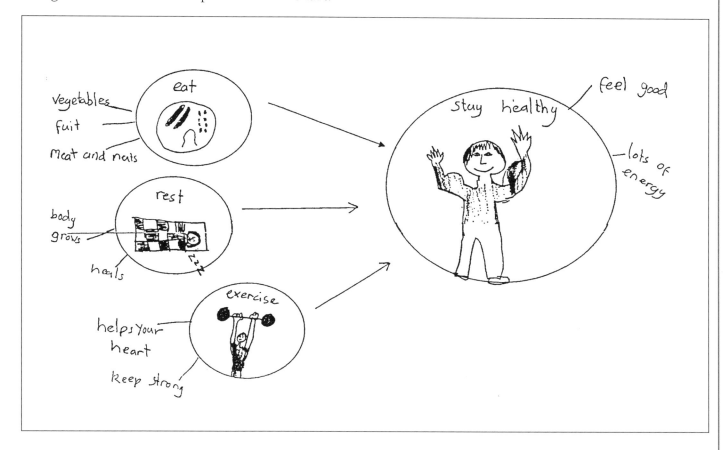

Discussion about the effects of exercise and rest
on the human body produced cycle flowcharts:

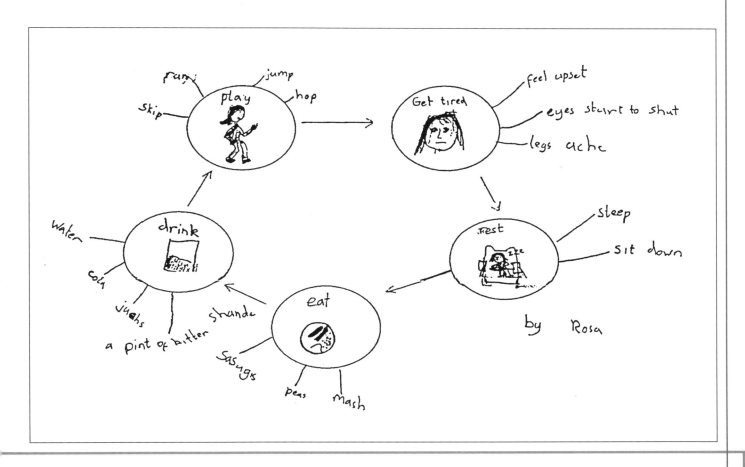

None of these flowcharts was used as a starting point for writing. Not only is explanation writing extremely difficult (especially for young children), it is often far less effective than a well-drawn diagram. Peter was using skeleton frameworks to familiarise pupils with common structures which underlie many cross-curricular topics – but particularly scientific ideas.

More ideas

The following list has been compiled from ideas from teachers all over the country who have used explanation flowcharts with their classes.

- An explanation skeleton does not have to be carefully designed and neatly made. A quick skeleton can be created on the board to accompany any explanation, and remind children of the key elements and 'make your thinking visible'. Frequent opportunities to view such diagrams will help children see how arrows can be used to indicate cause and effect, and spatial organisation to show the connections between events/ideas.
- Nor is it necessary to get your skeleton notes right first time. Children need to know that it is not easy to represent causal relationships – many are extremely complex, and it takes time to work out a clear visual explanation.
- Incorrect flowcharts are often as useful as successful ones. Peter Scott used the skeleton below, purportedly showing 'reversible change', to help children recognise that the car's cleanliness and shininess were irrelevant to whether it was moving or stationary.

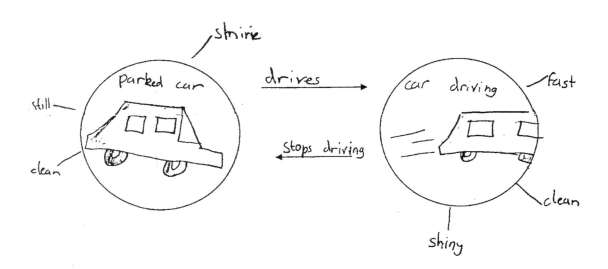

Teaching materials
8 Recount text

Characteristics of recount text

Purpose

To retell events in time order – 'a true story'

Text structure

- **orientation**: setting the scene — who, what, where, when?
- **sequential organisation** – what happened, in time order
- closing statement(s) – bringing the writing to a satisfactory conclusion
- basic skeleton framework – a **timeline** ('this happened, then this happened, etc.').

Language features

- **past** tense (specific events that only happened once)
- **time connectives** and other devices to aid chronological structure
- first- or third-person writing
- focus on **specific participants** (this often means **proper nouns**).

Key teaching points

- Recount is the most common type of non-fiction writing in Foundation and Key Stage 1 and includes: regular 'news' or diary writing; accounts of outings and holiday activities; 'true stories' of events in history or RE; and accurate reporting of classroom activities in science or other curriculum areas.
- Young children also need considerable help in organising information into **chronological order**. They often omit or confuse events, especially if facts or experiences are new to them. Preliminary organisation of the content as notes or pictures on a timeline can help

- children recognise which events are significant and see them as a visual sequence.
- Refer to your notes/pictures as 'memory joggers'; this will help the children when they come to write. You can then ask them to 'Turn each memory jogger into a sentence'.
- With older children, the completed timeline may also be used as a paragraph planner. Before they start to write ask them to draw red lines through the timeline to show where there is a natural break in the story. You can then suggest: 'When you come to a red line, miss a line in your book and start a new sentence.'

> **Common forms of recount text**
> - letter
> - biography or autobiography
> - diary or journal
> - newspaper or magazine report
> - non-fiction book (e.g. history)
> - encyclopaedia entry
> - write-up of a trip or activity
> - account of science experiment.

MY LIFE SO FAR

My name is Jessica Martin and I am six years old. I live in York with my mum and my little brother Baz. This is the story of my life so far.

I was born at St Mary's Hospital on 19th December, 1997. I was a good baby and did not keep Mum awake much at night. When I was 3, Baz was born. He was not a good baby! He cried all the time and kept us all awake.

Not long after Baz was born, I started at playgroup and met my best friend Hannah. We had lots of fun playing in the house and dressing up. At the age of 4, I had chicken pox. It made me very itchy and Mum dabbed my spots with pink medicine.

Soon after that, I started school. Hannah and I were in Mrs Robinson's class. It was fun because we played all day. Next we went into Mrs Bennett's class. That was when I learned to read and write. Mrs Bennett read us lots of stories.

Last September I moved up into Mr Long's class, and now I am learning my times tables.

Shared reading of 'My life so far'

The passage can be used for one or more of the following, depending on the children's age and ability.

Introducing timelines

Read the passage to the children then demonstrate how to turn the text into a timeline:

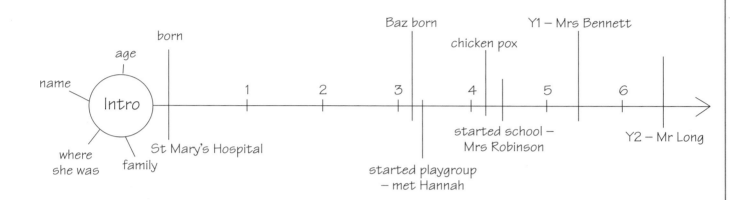

An introductory paragraph

Reread the introductory paragraph. This is report text, telling the reader some essential facts about the author before the life story begins. Establish that it covers name, age, where she lives, who is in her family. Use as a speaking frame for planning introductory paragraphs about the children themselves (see page 19):

'*My name is . . . and I am . . . years old. I live in . . . with . . . . This is the story of my life.*'

Ask the children to express the same information about themselves in other ways, always using sentences.

The language of time

Reread from the beginning of paragraph 2, where the piece becomes recount text.

Ask the children to look for ways in which the author shows time passing (shaded words) and collect on a poster:

● giving dates
● sentence openings like *When I was three . . .* and *At the age of four . . . .*
● simple time connectives: *next, now.*

Note that author never uses *then* and never uses the same expression twice. Discuss how these 'signposts' help the reader keep track of the life-story and show you that it is being written in time order. Over time, add further time connectives (and

other devices for showing the passage of time) to your poster, collected from other recount texts.

With older/more able pupils, ask them to reread the passage, a paragraph each. Help the children to mark paragraph breaks on the timeline, and note how paragraphs reflect the most significant events in Jessica's life.

Keeping the reader's interest

Help the children notice how Jessica structures her retelling – for each separate event, she states the fact, then gives at least one interesting detail, e.g.

Facts of her birth – she was a good baby.
Baz's birth – not a good baby!
Joined playgroup – fun with Hannah.
Chicken pox – pink medicine.

Older children could follow this structure in their own writing.

Capital letters for proper names

Ask the children to reread the passage, a sentence each. Highlight capital letters at the beginning of sentences. Discuss why other words have capital letters. Collect examples of names of people, places, months and forms of address (Mr, Mrs). Note also the use of capitals to make the title stand out.

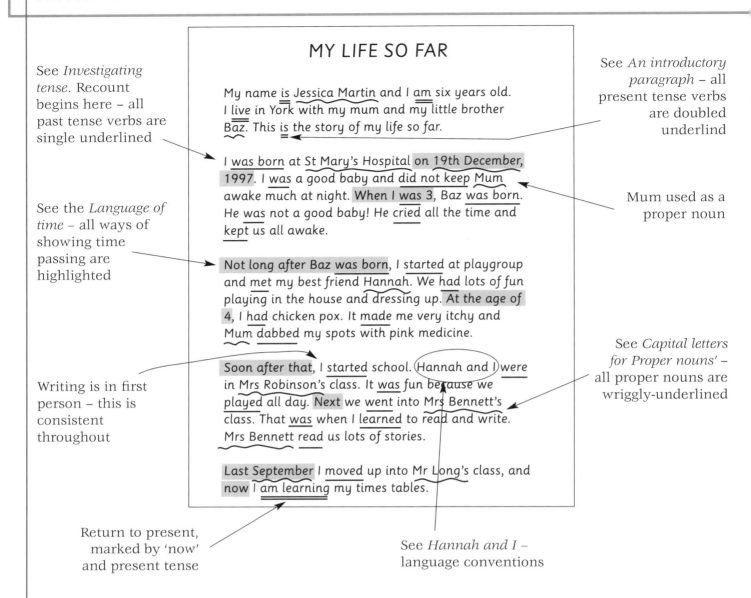

See *Investigating tense*. Recount begins here – all past tense verbs are single underlined

See the *Language of time* – all ways of showing time passing are highlighted

Writing is in first person – this is consistent throughout

Return to present, marked by 'now' and present tense

See *An introductory paragraph* – all present tense verbs are doubled underlind

Mum used as a proper noun

See *Capital letters for Proper nouns'* – all proper nouns are wriggly-underlined

See *Hannah and I* – language conventions

MY LIFE SO FAR

My name is Jessica Martin and I am six years old. I live in York with my mum and my little brother Baz. This is the story of my life so far.

I was born at St Mary's Hospital on 19th December, 1997. I was a good baby and did not keep Mum awake much at night. When I was 3, Baz was born. He was not a good baby! He cried all the time and kept us all awake.

Not long after Baz was born, I started at playgroup and met my best friend Hannah. We had lots of fun playing in the house and dressing up. At the age of 4, I had chicken pox. It made me very itchy and Mum dabbed my spots with pink medicine.

Soon after that, I started school. Hannah and I were in Mrs Robinson's class. It was fun because we played all day. Next we went into Mrs Bennett's class. That was when I learned to read and write. Mrs Bennett read us lots of stories.

Last September I moved up into Mr Long's class, and now I am learning my times tables.

(Note: the children do not need to know this, but just in case someone asks!) The word *Mum* is sometimes used as a proper noun (in which case it needs a capital), and sometimes as a common noun (as in paragraph one: *my mum*, like *my brother*).

Ask the children to state/write some proper nouns associated with themselves, which need capital letters.

Continue your collection of capital letters for proper nouns from your reading of other texts.

Investigating tense

Ask the children to reread the first two paragraphs. Can they spot that one is about 'now' and one is about 'the past'? How do they know where the change happens? Guide them to a recognition of the change of tense between *I live*

and *I was born*. Many of the verbs in the passage feature the –ed ending (there are also examples of all spelling rules associated with it: *cry – cried; dab – dabbed; move – moved*). Others are common irregular past tenses, and there are two examples of verb chains (*was born* and *did not keep*).

Regular past tense	*Irregular past tense*
cried dabbed learned started played moved	was met made went kept had were read

Hannah and I

In the penultimate paragraph, Jessica refers to *Hannah and I*. Explain that this is the conventional order when writing about yourself and another person (or persons). As well as being grammatical, it is also polite because you are putting the other person first.

Ask the children to work in pairs to think of two things they and their partner both like doing. They should then report back to the group using these speaking frames:

Partner 1:...and I both like....
Partner 2:...and I also enjoy....

Shared writing of 'My life so far'

A timeline frame for writing

Lesson 1: Collecting ideas and making a timeline
Talk about the children's own life stories and significant events and collect ideas for the sorts of things they might write about. Decide roughly how many events you want them to write about (each event should take one writing lesson).

The children are going to be writing their name, age, the place they live and about their family (those with very large families could write, e.g. *my mum, dad, 5 sisters* and *3 brothers*). Depending on the age/ability of the children you could, if necessary, verbally provide this information and check what they write through a 'show me' activity on individual whiteboards.

Demonstrate how to fill in a timeline for yourself (up to the age of five or six!). Then give each child a timeline frame (page 47) and help them write the information on it. Ask the children to take their timeline home to choose details to write about. Parents may also wish to send in photographs to help illustrate the finished piece of writing.

Lesson 2: Writing an introductory paragraph
Remind the children of the 'speaking frame' used earlier. Depending on the age/ability of the children, you may choose to use this for Shared Writing, or devise another way of presenting the information.

Write an introductory paragraph for yourself (aged 5). Demonstrate how to write the first sentence. Ask the children to compose the second sentence and scribe for them. Then ask them in pairs to compose and write a third sentence like the one in the original: 'This is the story of my life so far'. Choose one and scribe it. During Shared Writing, remind the children (as appropriate) about sentence-level features covered earlier, e.g. capital letters. Children should now write the title and introductory paragraph for their own life story.

Lesson 3: Telling the story
Remind children how each time you write a fact you write a sentence or so of detail about it. Provide a 'speaking frame' for the first sentence:

e.g. 'I was born at...on...' Ask the children to fill it in (see page 47). Model how to write your first paragraph in the same way as Jessica does – fact then detail; fact then detail. Use:

- demonstration writing for the first sentence
- scribing for the sentence of detail
- supported composition for the 'way of showing time passing' leading into the next fact.

Again, during Shared Writing, remind the children as appropriate about sentence-level features covered earlier, e.g. past tense.

Lessons 4, 5, etc.
Continue in the same way to continue the life story.

My life so far

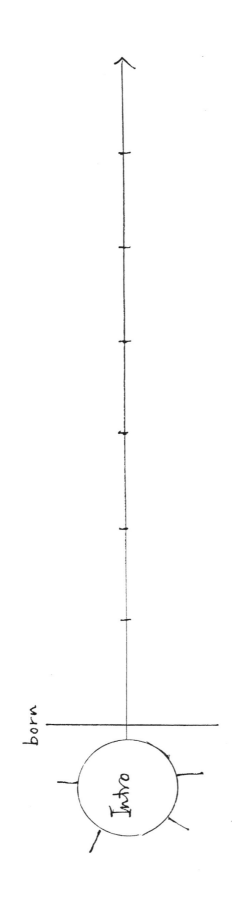

born

Intro

We are going to write our life stories. First we are going to plan them on a timeline (like the example below). Please will you help your child think of .... important events in .... life so far, and put 'memory joggers' on the timeline. Memory joggers can be words, phrases or even little pictures, as long as your child can remember what they stand for. Please talk about each event with your child and make sure .... knows some detail about it.

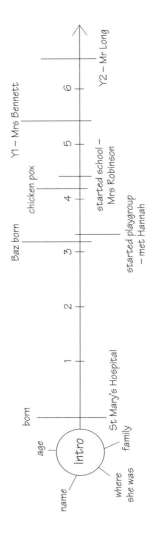

9 Instruction text

Characteristics of instruction text

Purpose

To tell someone how to do or make something

Text structure

- title or opening sets out **what's to be achieved**
- starts with **list** of items required
- often accompanied by **diagram(s)**
- sequenced steps to achieve the goal – what to do, **in time order**
- skeleton framework – a **flowchart** ('you do this, then you do this', etc.)

Language features

- **imperative** verbs ('bossy verbs')
- in time order (often **numbered** steps and/or **time connectives**)
- all necessary **detail** included (e.g. quantities, spatial directions)
- **clear, concise** language

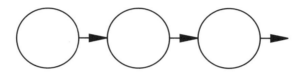

Key teaching points

- Simple instruction text is very direct, and thus fairly easy for young children to write. It is a useful vehicle for demonstrating major differences between the use of language in stories and in factual writing (e.g. descriptive language chosen for clarity, not vividness).
- It can also be used as a vehicle for focusing on verbs, as imperative verbs tend to be up at the front of the sentence. However, since the term 'imperative' is not very memorable for young children, it may be best to invent another (e.g. 'bossy verbs' was suggested by a Yorkshire teacher).

- It is very helpful if children can actually carry out the process concerned before they write. For this reason, cross-curricular links to art, DT, ICT, PE and so on are invaluable.
- Diagrams help make instructions clear. Children also need to be taught how to draw and label simple, clear diagrams.

Common forms of instruction text

- recipe
- technical manual (e.g. for car, computer)
- non-fiction book (e.g. sports skills, art)
- timetable, route finder
- list of rules
- posters, notices, signs
- sewing or knitting patterns
- instructions on packaging (e.g. cooking or washing instructions).

HOW TO MAKE A PERSONAL PHOTO FRAME

You will need:

A good photo of yourself
A rectangle of thick card, bigger than your photo
4 strips of thinner coloured card
Scissors
Glue
Coloured crayons or pens

1. Put the photo of yourself on the thick card, right in the middle. Use a dab of glue to stick it in position.

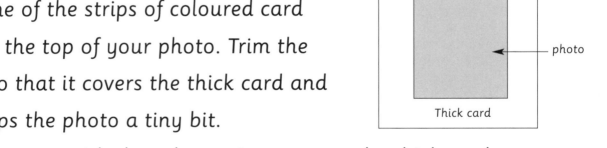

2. Lay one of the strips of coloured card across the top of your photo. Trim the strip so that it covers the thick card and overlaps the photo a tiny bit.

3. Do the same with the other strips to cover the thick card at the bottom and sides of the photo.

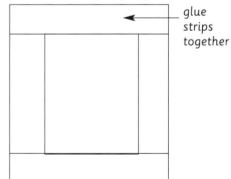

4. Glue the four strips together at the corners so they make a frame. Use coloured crayons or pens to decorate it with pictures of things you like.

5. Glue the frame over your photo on to the thick card.

6. Put your personal framed photo in the class display.

Shared reading of 'How to make a personal photo frame'

The passage can be used for one or more of the following, depending on the children's age and ability.

Following instructions

Unfortunately, the materials for this activity need a degree of preparation (cutting the backing card and coloured strips to the right size for making the frame). Young children will not be able to measure card strips, etc. for themselves, and the space available on a photocopiable A4 page limits the type of instructions that can be provided.

Read the instructions with the class, then provide the equipment and ask the children to follow the instructions to make their photo frames. If you are doing an 'Ourselves' topic, the photos can be integrated with the display.

Introducing flowcharts

Reread the instructions, then demonstrate how to turn them into a visual flowchart – pictures and memory jogger notes. Help the children to see that instructions are broken down into stages and organised in time sequence (like the timeline).

'Bossy' verbs

have made it more or fewer? (Warn children about the danger of splitting the process into too many steps.)

Cover the first word of each instruction with Post-its or blank-out tape. Invite the children to read the sentences, one at a time, and work out what the missing word might be. Reveal the word each time to check. As you work through the text, help the children to recognise that these words are all 'doing words'.

Introduce, or revise, the term 'verb' and explain that all sentences have verbs in them. Because instructions are all about telling you what to do, the verbs are very important so they're usually right up at the front of the sentence, 'bossing you about'.

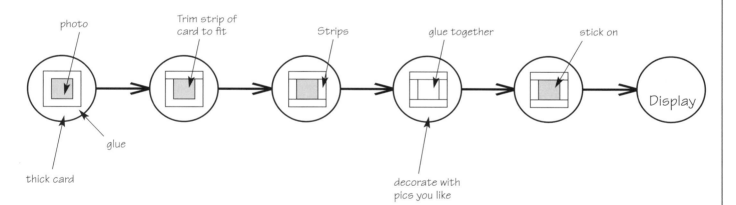

Numbered steps

Remind the children about timeline notes for 'life stories', and discuss how the skeleton framework for instructions is similar to and different from the timeline. Establish that either type of writing could be on either framework (since both show events in time order), but the flowchart is more suitable for instructions as it clearly breaks the process into steps.

Ask the children to reread the instruction passage, one step each. Discuss why the author has chosen to use numbers to signal the different stages in the process, rather than time connectives, as in a recount. Talk about why they have divided it up in this way: how might they have chosen the number of steps? Could they

Diagrams and labels

Cover up the captions on the diagrams in the large version of the instruction text. Can the children remember what they say? Reveal them and discuss why the labels are just words and phrases, rather than complete sentences. Discuss the importance of diagrams, helping children recognise that it is often easier to explain with a very simple labelled picture rather than in words. Explain that the lines connecting labels to diagrams are called 'leader lines' and should be drawn with a ruler.

Demonstrate how to draw and label a diagram (choose something related to the ongoing work of the class, or something familiar like an item of clothing). Ask children in pairs to try drawing a labelled diagram of a similar item.

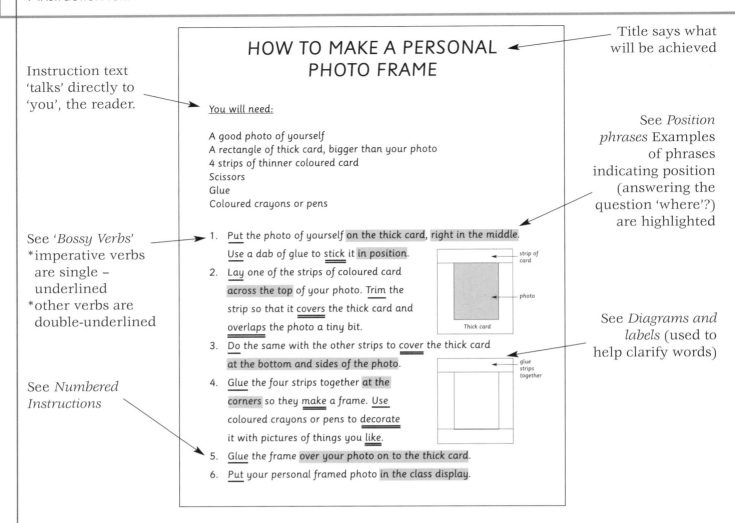

Instruction text 'talks' directly to 'you', the reader.

See 'Bossy Verbs'
*imperative verbs are single – underlined
*other verbs are double-underlined

See Numbered Instructions

Title says what will be achieved

See Position phrases Examples of phrases indicating position (answering the question 'where'?) are highlighted

See Diagrams and labels (used to help clarify words)

Position phrases

Return once more to the instruction text. Explain that in craft activities, such as making the photo frame, correct positioning of parts is very important. Ask the children to read the instructions, one sentence each, looking out for and highlighting phrases which answer the question 'Where?'. Collect good examples of these on a poster for future reference.

Shared writing: instructions for craft activities

Lesson 1: Talking about instructions
Note: to complete this activity – making a caterpillar – each child needs half an egg box. Enlarge the pictures on page 52 to share with the children. Talk about each one, establishing:

● that the first picture gives the list of equipment and the others are steps in the sequence of instructions for making a caterpillar
● the names of all the items of equipment
● what the child is doing in each picture
● that the stapler must be used by an adult.

Let the children follow the picture instructions to make their own caterpillars.

Lesson 2: Making memory jogger instructions
Soon after making the caterpillars, help the children make flowchart notes of what they did. Do not show the picture instructions.

Start by listing the items needed. Then discuss how you can jot down the first instruction (i.e. cutting the egg box in half). Children will probably want to draw it, but demonstrate how it's quicker (and easier) to write: *Cut box in half*. Demonstrate and scribe to make flowchart notes for the first three stages.

Talk about bossy verbs and any other sentence-level work you have covered through Shared Reading. Ask the children to copy the start of the flowchart, and then make their own notes to complete the instruction flowchart.

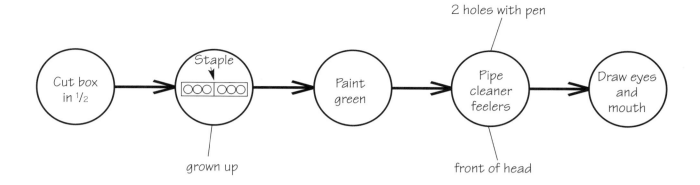

Lesson 3: Turning memory joggers into sentences
Use the visual prompt about instruction organisation on page 35 in section 6, 'Instruction Writing case studies', to remind the children of what is involved in writing instructions.

Ask them independently to write a title and a list of 'What you need', based on your notes for the last lesson. When most are ready, model how to use your skeleton notes to write up the first stage or two in the process, using a mixture of demonstration, scribing and supported composition. The children can then complete the writing of the instructions, in pairs or independently.

Lessons 4 + : Writing instructions independently
Provide materials and spoken directions for the children to make butterfly pictures by folding paper, painting a 'half-butterfly' on one side of the fold, then pressing the two sides together to make a symmetrical picture.

Ask them, in pairs, to:

● create a list of materials + flowchart notes for the activity
● use these to write instructions on 'How to make a butterfly picture'.

(The two craft activities suggested here link to the explanation writing activity section 11, Shared writing of 'How butterflies grow', p. 64).

How to make a caterpillar

10 Report text

Characteristics of report text

Purpose

To describe the characteristics of something

Text structure

- introductory information about what is to be described: who, what, when, where (overall classification)
- **non-chronological** organisation
- description organised according to **categories** of information
- basic skeleton framework – a **spidergram** (one spider-leg per category; this could divide into further spider-legs, depending on the degree of detail).

Language features

- **present** tense (except historical reports)
- usually general nouns and pronouns (not particular people or things)
- **third-person** writing
- factual writing, often involving **technical words** and phrases.

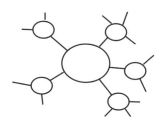

Key teaching points

- The difference between report and recount is that report text is usually non-chronological (although there are occasional reports which can be chronologically organised, e.g. a generalised *Day in the Life of . . .* which is not about a specific day or person). The basic skeletons for the two text types show this difference clearly.
- Learning to organise report text involves learning to categorise information. There are three stages in making a spidergram (which we have called BOSsing – described on page 30),

and many children find the process challenging. It is, however, worth the effort to teach it well, as categorisation is an important thinking skill. (See the spidergram 'Common forms of report text'.)
- There are other ways of representing report text (e.g. picture, labelled diagram, plan or map) which may be used instead of or in addition to the spidergram. Many reports are comparative, in which case a grid may be the most appropriate skeleton.

Common forms of report text

- information leaflet
- school project file
- tourist guide book
- encyclopaedia entry
- magazine article
- non-fiction book (e.g. geography)
- letter.

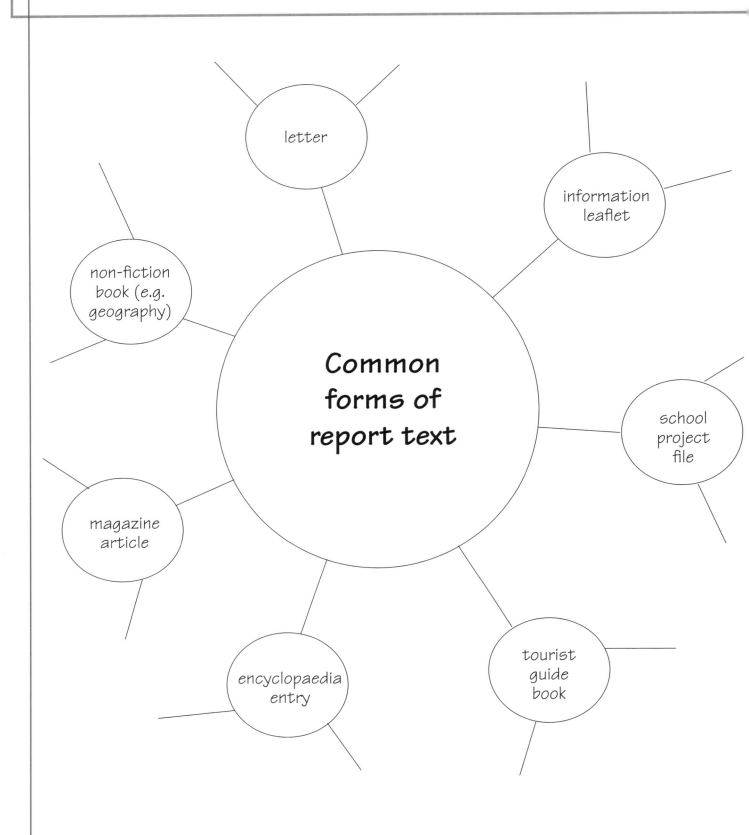

letter

information leaflet

non-fiction book (e.g. geography)

Common forms of report text

school project file

magazine article

encyclopaedia entry

tourist guide book

OUR SCHOOL

Our school is called Lee Park Primary, and it is in Longton near York. Lee Park has seven classes, from Reception to Year 6, and there are 198 pupils in the school. It was built in 1965.

Lee Park has a big playground, with special sections for the infants and the juniors. In the infant playground there are lots of shapes painted on the ground, like hopscotch squares and a map of Britain, for people to play on. There is also a special area for sitting quietly. The junior playground has play areas marked out as well, including football and netball pitches.

We also have a school field. This is next to the school down a little lane. In the summer we are allowed to play on the field too, but in winter it is too muddy. However, when it snows, Mrs Carr (our headteacher) sometimes lets us go on the field.

The school has a big school hall that we use for assembly and for some lessons, such as gym and drama. We also use the hall for lunches. You can bring packed lunch and sit at the back of the hall, or you can have a school lunch. The dinner ladies serve this on long wooden tables at the front of the hall. The rest of the time, the tables are stored in a cupboard.

Shared reading of 'Our school'

The passage can be used for one or more of the following activities, depending on the children's age and ability.

Making spidergrams

Read the passage to the children then demonstrate how to turn the text into a spidergram. Help the children to see that each paragraph (an arm of the spidergram) is about a particular topic.

Discuss how putting all the facts about a certain topic together helps the reader keep track of the details. Since descriptions are not written in time order, you need some way of organising all the information.

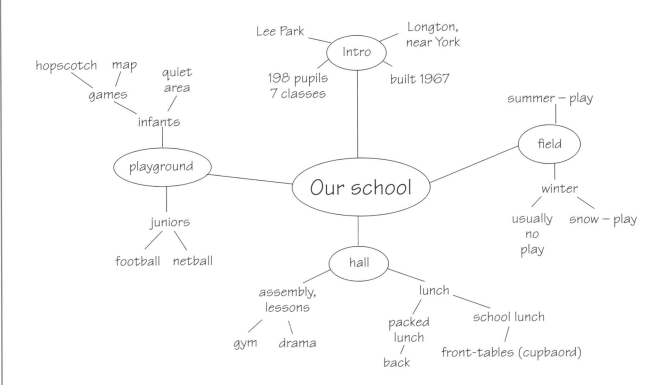

An introductory paragraph

Reread the introductory paragraph. This is report text, telling the reader some essential facts about the school as a whole. Establish that it covers the name, where it is, the number of classes and pupils and the date when it was built. Provide (or discuss or send children to research) the same facts for your school, and note them on the board. Use as a speaking frame for an introductory paragraph about your school (see page 19):

'Our school is called..., and it is in....
...has...classes, and there are...pupils in the school. It was built in....'.

Then ask the children in pairs to think of other ways of ordering the information into sentences. In seeking responses, stress a variety of sentence openings.

Sorting out information

Reread from the beginning of paragraph 2 and, without referring to your spidergram notes, ask the children what the main topic of each paragraph is. Note how the first words of each paragraph introduce the topic (see shaded words).

Display the spidergram and show how, from paragraph 2, the information in each paragraph is split into two parts – sometimes it's then split up even further. Appoint two children, an 'infant' and a 'junior', to read the first sentence of paragraph 2 like this:

Both: *Lee Park has a big playground, with special sections for*
Infant reader: *the infants*
Both: *and*
Junior reader: *the juniors.*

Ask pupils in pairs to appoint themselves 'infant' and 'junior' and read paragraph 2. 'Infant' should read all the bits about the infant playground, 'junior' should read all the bits about the junior playground. Get one pair to demonstrate, then discuss how the author makes it very clear which playground he or she is talking about (*In the infant playground....There is **also**.... The junior playground....*).

present tense for
report writing

one past tense
verb referring
to history

OUR SCHOOL

Our school is called Lee Park Primary, and it is in
Longton near York. Lee Park has seven classes, from
Reception to Year 6, and there are 198 pupils in the
school. It was built in 1965.

See *Sorting out
information.*
All topic sentences
are highlighted

Lee Park has a big playground, with special sections for
the infants and the juniors. In the infant playground
there are lots of shapes painted on the ground, like
hopscotch squares and a map of Britain, for people to
play on. There is also a special area for sitting quietly.
The junior playground has play areas marked out as
well, including football and netball pitches.

See *The Word And.*
'and' is underlined
throughout.
Other words
signalling extra
information are
double-underlined

See *Giving Examples.*
Words signalling
examples have
wiggly underlining

We also have a school field. This is next to the school
down a little lane. In the summer we are allowed to
play on the field too, but in winter it is too muddy.
However, when it snows, Mrs Carr (our headteacher)
sometimes lets us go on the field.

The school has a big school hall that we use for
assembly and for some lessons, such as gym and
drama. We also use the hall for lunches. You can bring
packed lunch and sit at the back of the hall, or you can
have a school lunch. The dinner ladies serve this on
long wooden tables at the front of the hall. The rest of
the time, the tables are stored in a cupboard.

capital letters for
proper nouns
(see activity for
Recount, page 44)

Over-use of the word *and*

Ask the children to reread the passage, a sentence
each, while the class watches out for the word *and*.
After each sentence, highlight all the *ands*. Help
the children note that, in writing, *and* is always in
the **middle** of the sentence, never at the
beginning (see page 73 in Appendix 3 on
Grammar). Talk about how *and* is used to link
ideas together but, if it is over-used, it can become
very boring. Now, using an enlarged copy of page
60, a slightly changed version of the 'Our school'
text, demonstrate the effects of over-using *and*. By
comparing this to our original text, help the
children see that the author has avoided these
problems in the original version by

- splitting the ideas up into sentences – no more
  than two ideas linked by *and* in any one sentence
- sometimes using other words to show that he or
  she is giving extra information: *too, as well, also.*

Help the children recognise that *and* is an
important word and we couldn't do without it, but
it should not be over-used.

Giving examples

Before rereading the passage, point out that, when
the author is describing aspects of the school, s/he
often gives examples to show what s/he means
more clearly. Can pupils spot occasions when this
is done? Draw attention to the examples and the
words (in bold below) that signal to the reader that
we are going to hear some examples.

> *. . . shapes painted on the ground, **like** hopscotch
> squares and a map of Britain . . .*
> *. . . play areas marked out as well, **including**
> football and netball pitches.*
> *. . . . some lessons, **such as** gym and drama.*

Provide the following speaking frames for pupils
to fill in (see page 19):

> Some of our class have long names, **like** . . . .
> There are many boys in our class,
> **including** . . . .
> Our class does lots of lessons, **such as** . . . .

Mention two other useful 'signal phrases' with which writers can start 'example sentences': *For example . . . . For instance . . . .*

Older or more able children should be able to think of sentences about other topics in which they can use the 'signal words' to introduce examples.

Shared writing: a class book about 'Our school'

Lesson 1: Writing an introductory paragraph
Remind the children of the 'speaking frame' used earlier. Depending on the age/ability of the children, you may choose to use this for Shared Writing, or devise another way of presenting all the information it covers.

Explain that you are going to write an introductory paragraph for a class book called 'Our school'. Demonstrate how to write a first sentence. Ask the children to compose a second sentence and scribe for them. Ask them, in pairs, to compose and write a third sentence. Choose one and scribe it. During Shared Writing remind the children, as appropriate, about sentence-level features covered earlier, e.g. capital letters. The children should now write their own introductory paragraphs. Pick the best of these to use in the class book.

Lesson 2: Finding out
Organise for groups to go on 'fact-finding walks' around the school, during which they can talk to each other and their group leader (teacher? classroom assistant? parent helper?) about the building and the facilities.

Lesson 3: Brainstorming
Ask the children to think of facts about the school that they think should be included in the book. Jot these in memory jogger form on individual Post-it notes, and stick them on a board. Discuss how you will group your ideas for writing, and draw a spidergram frame with labelled categories. Group the Post-its around the appropriate categories. Can the children think of more facts to put in each category? Add extra Post-its. Where there are several Post-its in a category, talk about ways you could create subcategories – draw extra spider-legs and regroup the Post-its.

Lesson 4: Turning memory joggers into sentences
Take one of the spidergram arms, and model how to write it up. Demonstrate how to turn one memory jogger into a sentence (or you may link two with *and*). Create more sentences through scribing and supported composition. Emphasise the aspects of composition you have covered in previous teaching.

In Independent Writing, ask:

- less able children to write up the paragraph you have just demonstrated
- other children to write up other paragraphs in the same way.

Choose the best to make a class book about 'Our school' and ask the children to illustrate it.

OUR SCHOOL
('and' version)

Our school is called Lee Park Primary, and it is in Longton near York and it has seven classes, from Reception to Year 6, and there are 198 pupils in the school and it was built in 1965.

Lee Park has a big playground, with special sections for the infants and the juniors and in the infant playground there are lots of shapes painted on the ground, like hopscotch squares and a map of Britain, for people to play on, and there is a special area for sitting quietly, and the junior playground has play areas marked out, including football and netball pitches.

And we also have a school field and this is next to the school down a little lane and in the summer we are allowed to play on the field too, but in winter it is too muddy. However, when it snows, Mrs Carr (our headteacher) sometimes lets us go on the field.

The school has a big school hall that we use for assembly and for some lessons, such as gym and drama, and we use the hall for lunches and you can bring packed lunch and sit at the back of the hall, or you can have a school lunch, and the dinner ladies serve this on long wooden tables at the front of the hall and, the rest of the time, the tables are stored in a cupboard.

11 Explanation text

Characteristics of explanation text

Purpose

To explain how or why something happens

Text structure

- the title often asks a question or defines the process to be explained
- the text usually opens with general statement(s) to introduce the topic
- a series of logical steps explain the process, usually in time order often accompanied by **diagram**(s)
- a basic skeleton framework is given – a **flowchart** ('this happens, leading to this, which leads to this', etc.).

Language features

- **present tense** (the process is general)
- **time connectives** and other devices to aid sequential structure
- **causal connectives** and other devices demonstrating **cause and effect**.

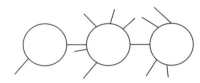

Key teaching points

- Explanations are very difficult to write, particularly for young children. Before putting pen to paper, children must thoroughly understand the process they are about to explain. Making a skeleton framework first – especially a flowchart and/or labelled diagram – develops understanding.
- However, even making the flowchart can be tricky! There are many possible variations, depending upon the process in question, e.g.:

- Children need to see plenty of models created by the teacher. They also need time to experiment with different ways of representing a process (collaborative work is particularly useful). However, the process of developing a suitable skeleton framework can in itself aid understanding.
- The language of explanation is also extremely difficult for many KS1 children, who are just getting to grips with the idea of cause and effect. They need plenty of opportunities to 'play with' words like *because, so, unless* and *if*.

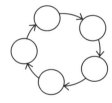
a **cycle**

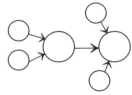
multiple causes and/or effects

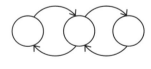
reversible effects

Forms of text which may be explanation text

- text book
- encyclopaedia entry
- non-fiction book (e.g. geography, biology)
- technical manual (e.g. for car, dishwasher)
- 'question and answer' articles and leaflets
- write-up of science experiment.

HOW DO BABIES GROW?

Newborn babies are very small. Most of them weigh round about 3½ kilograms and are only about 53 centimetres from head to toe. Some are even smaller. However, soon after they are born, babies are ready to eat! Their food is milk, which they suck from their mummy's breast or from a bottle.

The milk helps the baby grow, so by 3 months old it weighs about 6 kilograms and is around 60 centimetres long. Its tummy is growing stronger too. This means mum can give the baby some solid food as well as milk. The food is special mushy baby food because the baby does not have any teeth, so it cannot chew yet.

At 6 months old a baby is about 8 kilograms and 68 centimetres long. Its body is stronger now so it can sit up and play. Its little teeth are starting to come through. This means it can have some hard food like rusks as well as baby food and milk.

By one year old, most babies weigh around 9½ kilograms and measure about 72 cms. They can stand up, and will soon start to walk. They usually have several teeth, so they can eat the same food as older children, as long as it is cut up small. As they eat more and more, they will grow heavier, taller and stronger.

Shared reading of 'How do babies grow?'

The passage can be used for one or more of the following, depending on the children's age and ability.

Introducing flowcharts

Read the passage and demonstrate how to turn it into a flowchart. Help the children to see that each paragraph deals with the baby's development at a particular age, which becomes the stage in the sequence (a circle). Details about the baby at each stage can be added around the circle, as in a report spidergram.

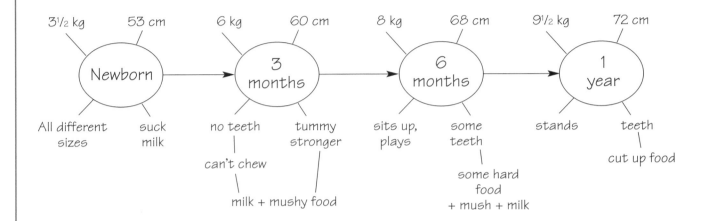

Cause and effect

Many children have difficulty with the language of cause and effect, and visual representations can be helpful in clarifying the concept. Talk about simple examples of cause and effect that are familiar to the children and represent them in skeleton form, e.g.:

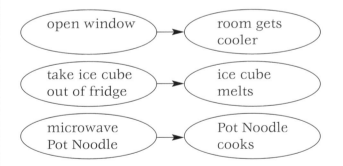

Discuss which is the cause and which is the effect in each case. Label them C and E.

Now introduce these speaking frames, and help the children work out how to fit each cause and effect into each frame.

1 When . . . . , ...
2 . . . . , so . . . .
3 . . . . This means that . . . .
4 . . . . because . . . .
5 The reason that . . . . is that . . . .

(1 When *I open the window, the room gets cooler*.)
(2 *I open the window*, so *the room gets cooler*.)
(3 *The window is open.* This means that *the room gets cooler.*)
(4 *The room gets cooler* because *the window is open.*)
(5 The reason that *the room gets cooler* is that *the window is open.*)

HOW DO BABIES GROW?

Newborn babies are very small. Most of them weigh round about 3¹/₂ kilograms and are only about 53 centimetres from head to toe. Some are even smaller. However, soon after they are born, babies are ready to eat! Their food is milk, which they suck from their mummy's breast or from a bottle.

The milk helps the baby grow, so by 3 months old it weighs about 6 kilograms and is around 60 centimetres long. Its tummy is growing stronger too. This means mum can give the baby some solid food as well as milk. The food is special mushy baby food because the baby does not have any teeth, so it cannot chew yet.

At 6 months old a baby is about 8 kilograms and 68 centimetres long. Its body is stronger now so it can sit up and play. Its little teeth are starting to come through. This means it can have some hard food like rusks as well as baby food and milk.

By one year old, most babies weigh around 9¹/₂ kilograms and measure about 72 cms. They can stand up, and will soon start to walk. They usually have several teeth, so they can eat the same food as older children, as long as it is cut up small. As they eat more and more, they will grow heavier, taller and stronger.

Explanation text is usually written in the present tense

See *Cause and effect* Examples of causal language are underlined

See *General Information* examples of words and phrases suggesting babies are all slightly different are wriggly-underlined

See *Organising Ideas* Highlighted section give patterned information

See *singular or plural* second and third paragraphs are written in the 'generalised singular'

Help the children see that, in the last two frames, the effect is mentioned before the cause. Reread the passage, looking out for and collecting examples of causal language. In each case, make a diagram like the ones above to show the cause and effect. One sentence contains two cause and effect constructions:

Organising ideas

Ask some children to reread the passage, one paragraph each. Can they see

- why the author has chosen to put the paragraph breaks where they are?
- a pattern in the way each paragraph is constructed (age, weight and length of baby; development and diet)?

Collect the four constructions which give information about age, weight and length (shaded

words) and help the children see that the author has tried to vary the way s/he presents these facts. Can they think of other ways of presenting the information each time (e.g. *When the baby is...; Three months later, the baby weighs...*)?

Singular or plural

Before rereading the passage again, ask the children whether the information is about babies in general or one baby in particular. How do they know this? (The usual answer is something like 'Because it says *babies*, not *baby*'.)

Ask some children to read the passage, a sentence each, to check whether this is true. Discuss the fact that the middle two paragraphs are actually written in the singular. This use of the 'generalised singular' can be confusing to young children. The technique allows writers to vary sentence construction (repetition of *babies* would become boring). However, it can lead to problems with gender (the use of *it* here sounds slightly odd, but a generalised baby does not have a gender, and repeated use of *he* or *she* would make sentences too complex for young readers).

Look in other non-fiction books for examples of this frequently used device e.g. ('The snail...',

'The caterpillar…') and ensure that children are not under the impression that these are specific snails, caterpillars, etc.

General information

Another difficulty for authors writing generalised information (e.g. reports and explanations) is that any descriptive detail must refer to an 'average': there will be variation between different examples of the 'specimens' under consideration. This means they need to convey the possibility of variation.

Ask some children to read the passage, a sentence each, checking for words and phrases that suggest that not all babies are the same (see wiggly underlining) and make a collection of these for future reference.

Keep an eye open for this type of language use in other report and explanation texts you read across the curriculum.

Shared writing of 'How butterflies grow'

Lesson 1: Making skeleton notes
Enlarge the six pictures of a butterfly's development (p. 66) to share with the children. Talk about each one, establishing what is happening at each stage in the butterfly's development. Help the children create an explanation flowchart.

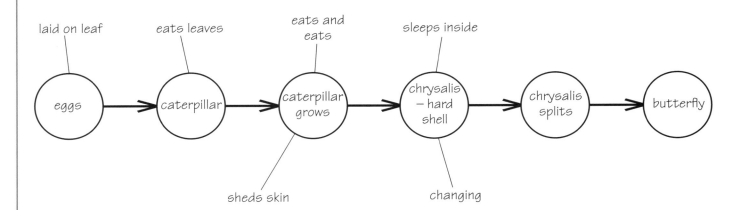

Establish that the adult butterfly is now able to lay more eggs, so the whole process begins again. Show how, in such a case, the flowchart can be converted into a cycle model.

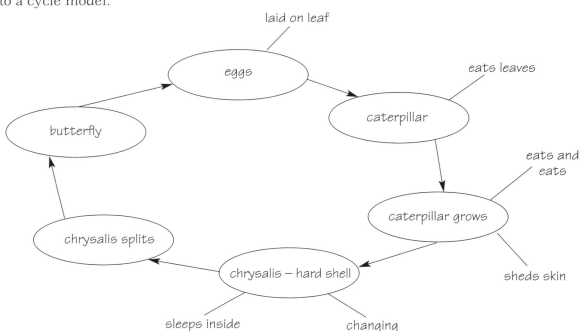

Lesson 2: Turning memory joggers into sentences
Model how to use your skeleton notes to write up

- the first stage in the process
- the beginning of the second stage.

Using a mixture of demonstration, scribing and supported composition, point out features of layout and language covered in earlier lessons. Children can then complete the writing of the explanation, in pairs or independently.

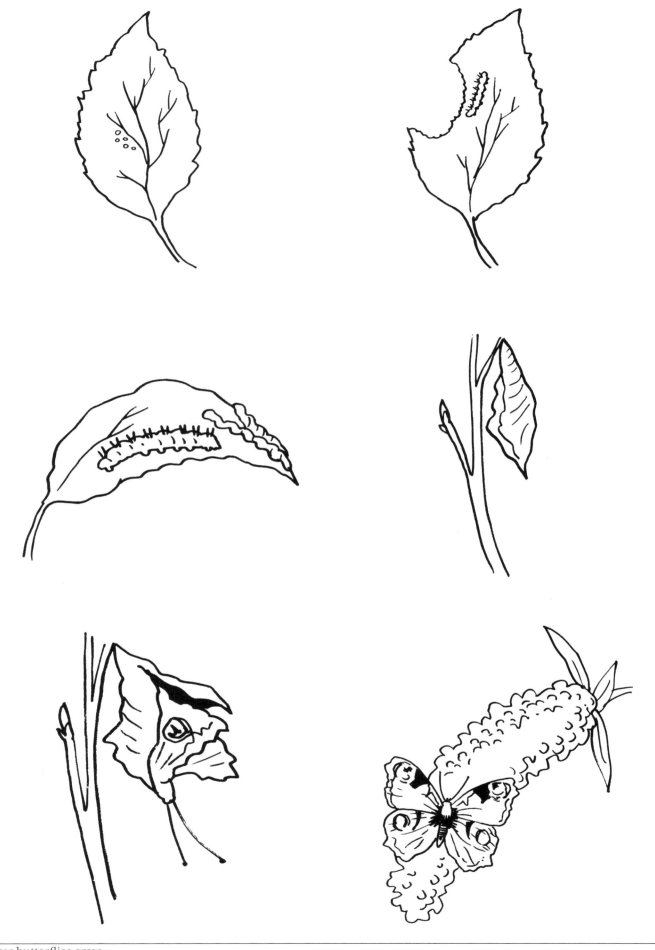

How butterflies grow

Appendices

1 Teaching phonics in Foundation and Key Stage 1

Much has been written in recent years about the teaching of phonics, and most schools now have schemes of work in place. The following checklist, based on a review of the third year of the National Literacy Strategy by HMI, may be helpful in ensuring that your approach is as effective as possible.

Effective phonics teaching is characterised by:

- good subject knowledge by teachers, including
  ○ using correct terminology with children
  ○ making constructive use of children's misconceptions in oral and written work
- a brisk pace of teaching
- rapid early coverage of letter–sound correspondences at the rate of several a week
- a focus on phonic skills (i.e. hearing, identifying, segmenting and blending sounds) as well as on phonic knowledge
- regular revision to consolidate learning
- an integrated approach to phonics and spelling – i.e. encoding is the reverse of decoding, but more difficult
- giving opportunities for pupils to apply their phonic knowledge and skills, especially in Shared Reading and Writing
- having a highly organised sequence of teaching, so it is clear exactly what follows what
- making effective use of teaching assistants
  ○ to support pupils in whole-class work
  ○ to provide separate phonics lessons for very young pupils in mixed-age classes
  ○ to provide catch-up help for those children who have fallen behind
- making effective use of schemes of work, including published materials.

If phonics is effectively taught alongside Shared Reading and Writing, it should soon become evident in children's writing development. The developmental checklist below, taken from the NLS materials for teaching assistants (2000), provides a guide to the normal developmental progression of handwriting and phonic skills. Progress can be considerably accelerated by appropriate teaching at each stage, geared to the next level of development.

- random scribble
- scribble that looks like writing
- individual shapes that look like letters
- some real letters used randomly (especially letters from own name)
- letters and shapes written from left to right across the page
- individual letters used to represent words (usually initial sounds)
- more than one letter used to represent a word (usually significant consonant sounds; in consonant–vowel–consonant (CVC) words, the first and last letters)
- some CVC words and key sight words spelled correctly (use of medial vowel in CVC words)
- simple regular words and key sight words usually spelled correctly.

Once children have achieved a reasonable level of writing competence, specific teaching can be based on learning objectives from the *NLS Framework of Objectives* (1997).

The four examples of writing on the following pages, based on the Goldilocks story, by children in the same Reception class, indicate different levels of development.

Illustrations courtesy of Di Hatchett, the National Literacy Strategy. Used with permission.

'What are you doing upstairs in my bed?'

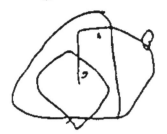

This child does not yet understand that pictures are different from writing or that letters are symbols rather than images. Specific teaching should focus on demonstrating that writing is a tool for communication, and showing that words are stable and read the same however often you read them, e.g:

- draw the child's attention to environmental print which provides information of interest and relevance to the child
- help the child learn to write his/her name
- through a little shared writing every day (e.g. sometimes just writing a label or a brief caption as well as longer sessions) demonstrate what writing is and what it is for
- develop phonological awareness (awareness of speech sounds) in preparation for more specific phonics teaching
- begin to introduce sounds through play (e.g. using a technique of associating a sound with an action).

'Get out of my bed!'

TO L oron B

This child has used recognisable letters that do not correspond to the phonemes in the words (the letters used may represent visual recall of writing on birthday cards or presents). Specific teaching should focus on developing appreciation of simple sound–symbol correspondences, e.g:

- general phonological awareness activities and phonic play
- systematic introduction of phonic sounds (e.g. the NLS *Progression in Phonics* activities)
- during Shared and Guided Reading and Writing, emphasise drawing attention to letter–sound correspondences at the beginnings of words
- games for developing awareness of initial sounds
- simple blending and segmenting games, to ensure that s/he doesn't become fixated on initial sounds.

'Get out of my house!'

GaOmh

This child has heard and written a symbol to represent the initial phoneme in each word, but has left no spaces between the words. He or she needs:

- systematic teaching of sound–symbol correspondences, ensuring coverage of one way to write each phoneme
- during Shared and Guided Reading and Writing, lots of attention paid to blending and segmenting of words
- games to sensitise him/her to final sounds in words
- help in recognising the spaces between words, and specific attention to this during Shared and Guided Writing (e.g. remembering to put 'finger-spaces').

'Don't come back!'

This child has discerned and represented the initial, final and medial phonemes in each word, but has not heard the 'n' of 'don't'. There are no spaces between the words and directionality may not be secure. Specific phonics teaching should focus on:

- systematic teaching of more advanced phonic knowledge (e.g. the NLS *Progression in Phonics*, step 4 onwards), including blending and segmenting of CCVC and CVCC words
- help to notice the spaces between the words.

However, while this fourth child is clearly ahead of his/her peers in phonic knowledge, there seems to be a real problem with handwriting. Unless help is given, the child's ability to recognise and remember sounds will outrun his/her ability to transcribe them. It is therefore essential that, alongside phonic skills, the teacher develops children's hand–eye coordination, hand control and ability to form letter shapes.

2 Teaching handwriting in Foundation and Key Stage 1

Preparing to write

The key to good handwriting is sound letter formation, and the National Literacy Strategy suggests teaching children three main hand movements (a curly **c**aterpillar for c, a long **l**adder for l, and a one-armed **r**obot for r) from early in the Foundation Stage. **However, this does not mean worksheets!** Children need to start with large-scale motor movements: writing with a stick or finger in the sand-tray; using paints, chalks or big felt pens to make colourful collages (a cabbage leaf full of curly caterpillars, for instance); and sky-writing the shapes, using their whole arm, right from the shoulder. There are many excellent suggestions for preparatory activities for handwriting in the *Penpals, Foundation 1* material by Budgell and Ruttle (see Appendix 5, page 77).

Learning the letter shapes

If they take part in plenty of preparatory activities, by the time children begin to learn about phonics in Reception, they should be familiar with the three critical movements upon which most letter shapes are based. Handwriting can then be taught alongside phonics, making use of the kinaesthetic learning channel to help children internalise the letter shapes that go with the sounds. Again, sky-writing and other large-scale practice is best to start with:

- introduce letters with big movements from the shoulder, using the whole arm
- next, move to finger-writing in the air
- when you feel that children have the hand control to do it confidently, let them try writing on wide-lined paper or whiteboards. (Lines are important because so much about handwriting is to do with letters' orientation to the line.)

Many children find it helpful if practice of a letter shape is accompanied by a familiar 'jingle'. For example, for letter A, 'Start at the caterpillar's head, come round his back, up to his head, drop to the line, and flick!' This can be pronounced rhythmically as the movements are made.

Always demonstrate letters so that children see the movements from the right direction – indeed, since this means turning your back on the class, it's usually better if you don't demonstrate yourself. Ask another adult (or a competent child) to stand at the front and demonstrate sky-writing then board-writing the letter, as you recite the jingle. This also frees you to watch how the children are coping, and to move among them

helping to adjust arm movements as they copy the demonstrator.

Dealing with difficulties

If some children lag behind the others in motor control, let them join in with the large-scale movements only (they can use magnetic letters when the others write), and provide plenty of opportunities for manipulative play (lacing, threading, cut-and-stick, construction toys, etc.) to develop hand–eye coordination. Ensure these children get extra help to catch up with handwriting as their motor skills develop.

Identify left-handed children as soon as possible. If children are undecided about handedness, try to guide them towards the right hand, as it will make their lives very much easier – but genuine left-handers will show a marked partiality which should be respected. Give extra help, modelling all practice movements and letter formations again for them using your own left hand (do this well away from the rest of the class!).

Keep an eye open for children who hold their pencils awkwardly. If possible, establish correct pencil grip from the moment children begin to use pencils for drawing and tracing. For those who can't remember the best way to hold the pencil, provide a commercial pencil gripper (such as a Stetro grip) for guidance.

Putting it into practice

To ensure children see the connection between forming letters and 'real-life writing', help them make the link between the letter shape (and its associated movement) and the initial phoneme of a word. For instance, once you have taught a number of letter shapes, hold up objects during shared word-level work, and ask the children to write the initial letter on their whiteboard.

In Shared Writing, demonstrate how to put this knowledge to use in writing words and sentences. Choose sentences that include the sounds/letters of the moment, and give a running commentary as you use phonics and letter formation to create words and sentences. Ask the class to have a go at a (carefully selected) word or phrase themselves, using their whiteboards – whiteboards are great for practising letters, because it doesn't matter if you make a mistake. As the children become more competent, you could give an occasional sentence as a dictation – this allows them to concentrate just on hearing the sounds and producing the letters, without the added burden of composition.

Linking handwriting, phonics and spelling

As phonics teaching progresses, use handwriting to mirror the phonic units you introduce; where two letters stand for one phoneme, teach them as a joined unit so that visual and kinaesthetic learning reinforce the idea of the digraph. Treating digraphs (two letters standing for one sound) and trigraphs (three letters standing for one sound) as handwriting units provides a powerful cognitive link when children are spelling out words phoneme by phoneme, e.g:

ch ee oo air

It also prepares the way for further joining of words as the children's fluency develops. For instance, it is very helpful to use joined writing for some high-frequency irregular words too, to reinforce the fact that these words should be remembered as wholes. Children can usually learn to write *the* as a whole word quite easily, and it is then a small step to writing *they* as a whole. The spelling of *they* creates difficulties for many children, and early establishment of a kinaesthetic model of the word would be helpful.

he → the → they

High-frequency words can be taught in this way in groups as children's hand control develops:

he   the   my   or   come
she   they   you   for   some
me   there   your   are

one   was   said   from
done   want
gone

As children's reading skills progress, they move from phoneme-by-phoneme spelling to processing words in larger chunks (such as onset and rime, e.g. ch-air, str-eam). This can be reflected in handwriting terms by increasingly treating common letter strings as joined units e.g:

ing and all old

As you teach the children how to join more and more letter strings and words, you can encourage them to use the same joins in their own writing.

Handwriting and spelling can continue to go hand in hand as the children's skills increase. Short snappy lessons are best, each concentrating on a group of words with a similar sound and/or spelling pattern. This is an ideal opportunity to revise and review phonic knowledge and high-frequency words. Short dictations featuring familiar words are also very valuable, as they allow children to concentrate just on spelling and handwriting, without worrying about what to write.

Handwriting practice

Children also need occasional opportunities to concentrate exclusively on handwriting, to practise joins, neatness and fluency. Patterns can be helpful, and sentences featuring all the letters of the alphabet are useful copybook exercises. With your help, children can make up more examples for themselves. They will also benefit from occasional copying of favourite poems or other extracts.

Handwriting comfort

When writing, a child's feet should be comfortably on the ground and his/her forearm resting on the table. The non-writing hand should rest on the paper to steady it. Seat left-handers so the movement of their arm does not clash with the right-arm movement of a right-handed child. All children should have a clear view of the board on which letter formation is demonstrated, and should not have to twist in their seat to watch or copy.

3 Teaching grammar in Key Stage 1

Learning to write does not come naturally in the same way as learning to speak. It involves many complex layers of skills, knowledge and concepts, the foundations of which are laid in Key Stage 1. One very important aspect of learning to write is a growing awareness of the grammar of our language.

Children don't need to know what sentences are in order to produce them in speech. But they do need to know in order to **write** them, to punctuate them and gradually to increase their control over ways of constructing them to express and explore their ideas. In the same way, awareness of basic word classes is totally unnecessary for speech, but helpful for understanding spelling rules, like adding -ed and -ing to verbs. And knowing a range of words for connecting ideas together can help move children away from the perennial 'and then... and then... and then' of spoken language.

At KS1, teaching is about developing general awareness rather than introducing technical grammatical language. But, in order to develop awareness, teachers must know what is important, and that involves understanding some grammatical terminology themselves. This appendix covers some of the basic information all KS1 teachers need to know about grammar.

What is a sentence?

As all teachers know, it is extremely difficult to define a sentence. One reason for this is that sentences are not important in spoken language. When we speak, it is usually interactive – two or more people tossing words and phrases back and forth, developing understanding as they go. Spoken language (particularly young children's spoken language) therefore tends to be quite disorganised, fragmented and interspersed with time-fillers such as 'like', 'sort of' and 'errrm'.

In writing, however, ideas must be much more carefully organised. The writer is on his or her own, conveying information without interaction – sometimes without even knowing who the audience will be. This means that carefully formed sentences are an important feature of written language patterns. We have to help children move from the disorganised, fragmented patterns of spoken language to the organised, sentence-based patterns of writing.

We can start introducing children to written language patterns as soon as possible by ensuring that they **hear** lots of written language – every time we read to children we are giving them experience of carefully constructed sentences. We

can also take every opportunity, in Shared Reading and Writing, to **demonstrate** what sentences are and **talk about** how they help texts make sense, for instance:

- by highlighting or writing each sentence of a text in a different colour
- by asking children to read a familiar text round a group, one sentence each
- by giving the gist of a sentence from a book in oral 'note form' and asking children to identify and read the 'complete sentence'.

During shared-skills teaching, we can **show how sentences are made** using concrete materials, e.g. words and phrases written on cards, held by children to create human sentences, or arranged on a washing line, Velcro strip or other sequencing device.

Filling in the detail

When we are speaking, we are usually in the same place as our audience, and we usually know something about them. This means we can take a lot for granted. We can make assumptions about shared knowledge, let background detail go through 'on the nod', impart information by gesture and tone of voice.

Young children's spoken language is particularly implicit. They assume their audience knows what they are talking about and, since their vocabulary is as yet undeveloped, they seldom provide much detail. We can help develop an eye (and ear) for detail by activities such as:

- providing interesting artefacts to talk about and collecting words about them
- playing 'talking games', e.g. one child describes a picture that his/her friends cannot see
- asking children to draw a picture of something they have done, then talking about it, drawing out details of what everything looked like, where and when it happened, what it felt like
- putting up a poster with the words *Who? What? When? Where? How? What were your feelings?* as an aide memoire to remind children of the importance of background detail during class talk
- using drama, role-play and puppetry to enhance children's awareness of background detail through experience.

Written language patterns

When we are speaking, there isn't time to think very carefully about the way we organise our words. We tend to state what happened fairly baldly, then add in any necessary detail afterwards. In writing, this can seem terribly repetitive so good writers use a variety of sentence structures to maintain their readers' interest. This involves varying

- sentence length – some long sentences, some short ones
- sentence type – occasional use of questions or exclamations
- word order, e.g. in these sentences, the words and phrases given in bold (which answer the questions *How? When?* and *Where?*), can all be moved around to create different emphases and effects:

> **Last night**/*the dog barked*/**loudly**/**in the back garden.**
> *The baby cried*/**miserably**/**for hours**/**in his cot.**

In Shared Reading, we can draw attention to how authors vary sentence length by using highlighter pens or tape. In Shared Writing, we can demonstrate how to use questions or exclamations to add interest, e.g.

> *What was she to do?*
> *What a surprise!*

We can also build up awareness of sentence variety during skills work, e.g.

- by giving a basic sentence such as *The children waited* or *The ghost wailed* for children to improve it by answering the questions *How? When? Where?*
- by using human sentences or words and phrases on a washing line, to show how you can move *How? When?* and *Where?* chunks around, to improve the sound of your sentence.

Joined-up thinking

As children develop greater control over language, they are ready to express increasingly complex ideas. Longer stories, for instance, usually involve a sequence of events. In spoken language, sequence is shown very simply by the linking words 'and then... and then... and then...'. In written language this sounds repetitive and boring, so children need to build up a repertoire of time connectives.

As time goes on, they will be ready to express other relationships between ideas, e.g. cause and effect, and condition. To do this effectively in writing, they need to construct complex sentences, linking their ideas with conjunctions such as *because, although, unless, until*, which encapsulate highly complex ideas. Children need opportunities to meet them in context and to practise using them to link ideas. (This is why, in

order to achieve a Level 3 in the SATs, children must 'join sentences with conjunctions other than *and* or *but*'.)

As well as using complex sentences, children will begin to write longer and longer texts. These texts must be 'cohesive' – that is, they must hold together, making complete sense to the reader. One important aspect of cohesion is consistency – if a piece of writing starts in the past tense, it should not drift into the present; if it starts in the first person (*I*), it should not drift into a third-person account (*he* or *she*).

In Shared Writing you can demonstrate how to repeatedly and cumulatively reread your work, checking that it makes sense and 'sounds right'. A poster like the one on page 20 can be used to encourage children to do this too.

Longer texts also need **sentence connectives** – words which make links **between** sentences in the same way that conjunctions make links between clauses. We have already mentioned sequential connectives (like *next* and *then*). Some more able children may begin to use logical connectives such as *However* and *Therefore*.

And... But... Or... So...

A common problem mentioned by teachers is that children often want to start sentences with the words *And, But, Or* or *So*. Technically speaking, these are coordinating conjunctions which should always occur in the middle of a sentence, linking two clauses. In written language, they should not be used to start a sentence. However, when writing informally (e.g. when writing for children), authors often mirror spoken language patterns, and thus do begin sentences with *And... But... Or... So...*. Children therefore see plenty of examples of this usage, and want to copy it.

With young children, the only answer is to explain that grown-up authors are sometimes allowed to break the rules, but in KS1 we must stick to them, to make sure we know the 'correct' way of writing. However, as children become more aware of language, you could put up a poster showing some formal equivalents of *and, but, or* and *so*:

And – Also	*So – Therefore*
But – However	*Or – On the other hand*

If children want to start a sentence with one of the coordinating conjunctions, they can see whether the formal word would do instead.

Punctuation

As children begin to write at greater length, they need increasing control over punctuation. In spoken language we can use our voices to make meaning clear – conveying where one 'chunk of meaning' ends and another begins by making tiny pauses or changes in tone or pitch. In written language, the only substitute for the voice is a system of dots, dashes and squiggles which mean very little to children.

It is therefore very important to take every opportunity to draw attention to punctuation and how it affects how we read. The main functions of punctuation relevant in KS1 are:

- it conveys grammatical boundaries, helping to make meaning clear (full stop, comma, dash)
- it can convey tone of voice (as for a question or exclamation)
- in narrative, it clarifies which text is direct speech and which is not (speech marks).

Standard English

Many children come to school speaking a regional or ethnic dialect of English, rather than the standard version in which they learn to read and write. If we suggest this non-standard English is somehow 'wrong' or 'inferior', we could offend both the children and their parents. It is therefore important to be clear about what standard English is, and why we teach it.

Standard English has its roots in the dialect spoken 500 years ago in the southeast of England, at the time of the first printing presses. This dialect became the form of language in which our written heritage – literature and learning – was encoded, as well as the dialect of our institutions (government, the law, education). All children therefore have a right to know their 'national dialect'. Without it they would be disadvantaged in formal social situations, and would have difficulty expressing themselves in writing.

Standard English may be spoken in any accent. It differs from dialect forms in terms of vocabulary and grammar, but other dialect grammars are just as valid in other social contexts. In a dialect-speaking home, it would be just as correct to say 'We was going on us holidays', as it would be to write 'We were going on our holidays' in school. Dialect grammars are *non-standard*, **not** sub-standard.

Dialect grammar is different in different parts of the country. It is helpful to keep a note of any non-standard forms used by children in the class. You can then draw attention to these forms and their standard equivalents when the topic arises (without drawing attention to particular children's usage). When a child speaks to you in non-standard English, the best response is to repeat the words in a natural voice, adjusting it to standard. Teachers should also always provide a model of standard English usage in their own speech.

For a complete interactive grammar course, see the NLS Grammar website: www.standards.dfes.gov.uk/literacy/prof-dev/?pd=ed

4 Case study materials

Tom Bowker's Eve

Long long ago, on a stormy winter's night, one man saved a whole town from starvation. This is the story of Tom Bowker, who braved the storms to snatch food from the sea.

In the far south-west of England, the county of Cornwall sticks out like a foot into the Atlantic Ocean. Near the very tip of Cornwall's toe is the little town of Mousehole, (or 'Mowsul' as the Cornish people say it). It got its name from the way fishing boats ventured out from the harbour into stormy seas, then scurried back like mice into their hole, bringing fish for the townsfolk to eat.

Then one year the storms were so bad that no boats dared leave the shelter of the harbour walls. Huge waves lashed the quayside, and people cowered in their houses, growing hungrier and hungrier. As Christmas drew near, children sobbed for want of food, starvation stalked the town, and still the storms raged.

At last, on 23rd December, Tom Bowker battled through the rain to his fishing boat. Other men volunteered to go with him, but he turned them away: they had families, while Tom had none. As dusk fell, there was a lull in the storm... and Tom cast off into the dark seas, throwing his nets into the waves. Then the storm swelled again, and the people of Mousehole, praying for his safe return, put lamps in their windows to light him back.

By some miracle, Tom's boat survived. The lights guided him home and the villagers rushed to help drag his catch up on to the quay. They made a special pie that night, a pie of many fishes, and named it Star-Gazy Pie after the lights that had twinkled all over Mousehole. And the townsfolk gave thanks for the hero who had saved them from starvation.

Now, every 23rd December Mousehole celebrates Tom Bowker's Eve. The town and harbour are festooned with lights, and everyone goes down to the Ship Inn on the quay, for a special meal of Star-Gazy Pie.

newborn

six weeks

three months

six months

one year

two years

	Newborn	6 weeks	3 months	6 months	1 year	2 years
Average weight	3½ kg	4 kg	6 kg	8 kg	9½ kg	13 kg
Average height	53 cm	55 cm	60 cm	68 cm	72 cm	86 cm

How do babies grow?

5 Teacher resources for cross-curricular writing

Materials from the National Literacy Strategy, available from Prolog: 0845 6022260

NLS Framework of Objectives (loose-leaf folder, 1997) (ref: NLST)

Developing Early Writing (book, 2001) (ref: DfEE 0055/2001)

Developing Early Writing (video, 2001)

Progression in Phonics (booklet with CDRom, 2000)

NLS NF Text Level Work: Activity Resource Bank Oxford University Press: 01536 741171

Up-to-date information on how to obtain copies of these and other NLS publications is provided on the NLS website: www.standards.dfes.gov.uk/literacy/publications

Other materials

The Key Stage 1 Skeleton Poster Book, Sue Palmer. TTS Group Limited: 0800 318686 (Other Skeleton Poster Books available)

Speaking and Listening at KS1 and KS2, QCA (revised edition). QCA: 01787 884444

QCA schemes of work for KS1 (with literacy links). www.qca.org.uk

HMI Review of NLS, the Third Year (ref: HMI 332). Ofsted: 020 7421 6800, or www.ofsted.gov.uk

Mind Your Head (Get to Know Your Brain and How to Learn), Heather Thompson and Sean Maguire. North-Eastern Education and Library Board: 028 9448 2200

Information Texts 1 (KS1); Information Texts 2 (KS2); First Steps NLS Edition + associated training. All from First Steps (Reed Education) 01865 888020

The Articulate Classroom: Talking and Learning in the Primary School, ed. Prue Goodwin. David Fulton Publishers: 0207 405 5606

Thinking Skills and Eye Q, O. Caviglioli, I. Harris and B. Tindall. Network Educational Press: 01785 225515

Drama (Key Stage 1), Larraine Harrison. Scholastic Ltd: 01926 813910

A Corner to Learn, Neil Griffiths. Nelson Thornes: 01242 267280

Puppet Talk, Lillian Coppack. TTS Group Limited: 0800 318686

Helping Young Children to Listen, Helping Young Children to Imagine, Lines of Enquiry. All by Ros Bayley and Lynn Broadbent. Lawrence Educational Publications: 01922 643833

Materials mentioned in this book

Kidspiration (CDRom). TAG Learning: 01474 537886

Induction Materials for Teaching Assistants (Teaching Assistants File) (2000). DfES.

How Babies Grow, Bobby Neate and Susan Henry. Longman

Penpals, Foundation 1, Gill Budgell and Kate Ruttle. Cambridge University Press.

Garden Crafts
for children

Garden Crafts
for children

❀❀❀❀❀❀❀❀❀❀❀❀❀❀❀❀❀❀❀

35 FUN PROJECTS
FOR CHILDREN TO SOW, GROW, AND MAKE

Dawn Isaac

CICO BOOKS
LONDON NEW YORK

For Ava, Oscar, Archie, and the Hail Weston Pre-School gardeners.

Published in 2012 by CICO Books
An imprint of Ryland Peters & Small Ltd
20–21 Jockey's Fields
London WC1R 4BW
519 Broadway, 5th Floor
New York, NY 10012

www.cicobooks.com

10 9 8 7 6 5 4 3 2 1

Text © Dawn Isaac 2012
Design and photography © CICO Books
2012

A CIP catalog record for this book is
available from the Library of Congress
and the British Library.

ISBN: 978 1 908170 25 5
Printed in China

Editor: Caroline West
Design concept: Emma Forge
Designer: Elizabeth Healey
Photographers: Emma Mitchell and
Martin Norris
Stylist: Sophie Martell

For digital editions, visit
www.cicobooks.com/apps.php

Contents

introduction

Gardening has always been a perfect children's activity. It combines muck and magic, a chance to get messy, and the promise of great things from even the tiniest seed. This book is designed to inspire in children a love of all things gardening. As well as exciting but achievable growing projects, there are also beautiful craft ideas that use items gathered from the garden and outdoors.

As the large family garden is a rarity these days, the vast majority of projects in this book can be created with almost no outside space at all. Even a sunny kitchen windowsill can give a child the chance to grow a whole range of herbs, salads, and flowers—and, what's more, they can keep an eye on progress while they munch on their breakfast.

The projects include lists of all materials needed as well as step-by-step instructions and photographs, making them easy for children to follow. The range of ideas means that there are plenty of simple projects to fill a quick 20 minutes, as well as more complex ones that will keep children occupied for an entire afternoon.

Perhaps more importantly, while children may think they are simply having fun, they will also be learning about gardening, from topics such as seed sowing and the germination process to the thinning out of crops and the importance of pollinators.

The basic techniques that children will learn in these projects can be used again and again. As their confidence grows, so their imagination and natural curiosity will hopefully lead them to explore this hobby further, perhaps in adapting some of the project ideas, taking part in a school gardening club, or even creating a small garden of their own.

sowing and growing

Children love to watch seeds sprout and then go on to develop into flourishing plants for the garden. For the best results, help them to sow, grow on, and care for their seeds, as well as maintain new plants in a little plot of their own.

Buying seeds

The cost of buying different types of seed can soon add up, so why not consider sharing the costs and splitting the packets with some gardening friends? If you do this, make sure you both have copies of the growing instructions from the back of the seed packets and remember to store the seeds somewhere cool, dark, and dry.

Potting mix

You can buy special seed potting mix, but most general-purpose potting mixes will do the job just fine. Do make sure you firm the potting mix down before and after sowing, though, so that it's in contact with the seeds.

Pricking out

Once your seeds have germinated, you will see some simple seed leaves form and after that a pair of "true leaves," which usually look a little different. At this stage, you can prick out the seedlings, which simply means moving them on to individual cells or pots where they have more room to grow.

To do this, hold the leaves very gently and loosen the potting mix around the roots with an old pen, small dibber, or even your finger until you can easily lift the seedling from the potting mix. Make a hole in a small potting-mix-filled pot or seed tray cell, and carefully lower in your seedling roots before covering them over with potting mix and firming it down.

Potting on

When a plant is becoming too big for its pot, you can "pot it on" to the next size up. Do this by gently squeezing the sides of the pot to loosen it, then place your hand over the top of the container, either side of the stem, and tip it upside down. You may need to pat the bottom of the pot to get it to release the plant. Next, place the plant in a larger container, already partly filled with potting mix, fill around the sides with more potting mix, firm it down, and give it a good watering.

Planting out

Make sure that you give your plant a good drink of water about an hour before you begin planting. Then prepare your planting hole by digging a space twice as wide as the plant, forking over the bottom and giving it a good watering. Take your plant carefully out of its pot, place it in the hole, making sure it is planted at the same depth as it was in the pot, backfill with the soil and firm it down well. Then, you guessed it, give it another good watering.

Watering

You will need to water seedlings and plants in pots very regularly if the weather is dry. The best time to water is early morning and evening because less water will evaporate in the sun in this way. Of course, if you see your plants wilting and flagging in the heat, then don't wait!

If plants are in beds, try watering by placing a garden hose on the ground and letting water slowly trickle out of it until the bed is well soaked. This keeps water off the leaves and allows it to gradually soak into the soil. In general, a thorough watering once a week is better than a little bit every day because it encourages plants to develop roots deeper in the ground, which helps them to withstand dry spells.

above If you are going to grow plants such as herbs that like free-draining conditions, then fork in some coarse sand or horticultural grit to the soil when preparing your beds.

above right: Rake over the soil before planting your beds and borders. This gives the soil a nice, crumbly texture and ensures that your plants will flourish once planted.

Try to have a watering can with a fine rose (the part with holes at the end of the spout) so that it pours a very gentle shower, which is less likely to wash away small seedlings. You can also water seed trays and plant pots by standing them in a bowl of shallow water for about 15–30 minutes (the larger the pot, the longer you leave it).

The right soil

If you are lucky enough to have a garden, why not give your child a little patch of their own for sowing and planting? It doesn't have to be very big; most of the outdoor projects in the book take up very little space, but try to find a sunny plot with good soil.

Soils differ immensely. The one thing that all soils have in common is that they can always be improved by adding organic matter, such as well-rotted manure or garden compost. Try to dig this in during the fall ready for planting the

following spring. This will give the worms and weather a chance to work all that goodness into the soil.

Preparing the soil

Just before planting, it is worth digging over the soil. Do this when the ground isn't wet. Soil is more delicate than you think and walking on it when it's wet can damage its structure.

Use a fork to lift and turn the soil, and then use the back of the tines (the pointed bits) to beat large clods of earth and break them up. At the same time, you need to be taking out any weeds and large stones that you find.

Once you have turned over the soil, tread it in gently. This involves shuffling up and down the soil like a penguin, using your feet to firm it down and get rid of large air holes. You can then use a garden rake to level the soil and create a nice crumbly texture, which is ideal for seed sowing.

containers

Container gardening is perfect for tiny hands and a wonderful solution if you only have a tiny backyard or balcony on which to grow an array of ornamental and edible plants in pots, window boxes, and recycled planters.

Drilling

This book includes lots of projects that make unusual planters out of different objects. Some, such as colanders, already have the holes that are essential for allowing excess water to drain away. For those that don't, you will need to create some for your children.

Most materials can be drilled. Wood is easily tackled with standard drill bits, and ⅜in (8mm) or larger is a good size to work with. Although metal can be drilled, you can also use a large nail and a hammer to make holes. Ceramic can be punctured with a specialty ceramic drill bit. It's also possible to use a masonry drill bit, although this will take longer.

With metal, ceramic, or any shiny surface, putting masking tape across the area before drilling will help prevent the drill bit from slipping. You should also make sure that the object to be drilled is held in a vice or secured in some way.

Plant pots

Plastic plant pots are very useful and can easily be recycled. Be careful, though, to give them a good clean with warm, soapy water to get rid of any potential plant pests and diseases.

You can also make pots of your own from recycled materials. Old cardboard inner tubes, with newspaper used to seal the ends, are excellent for starting off larger seeds, such as those of peas, beans, and even sunflowers, which need lots of room for their roots to grow. You can even make your own newspaper plant pots using a wooden plant-pot press.

Saving water

Pots and containers dry out very quickly, especially in warm weather. As well as keeping them regularly watered, you can also add some special water-retaining granules to the potting mix. These granules enable the potting mix to keep hold of the moisture for longer, which helps thirsty plants.

You can also assist water retention by lining pots with plastic. A good source of this is old potting mix bags, which can be recycled as liners. Simply cut the bag to the required shape and then puncture it by using a fork or snipping holes with scissors. This means that if the soil gets too wet, the water can escape rather than filling up the pot and drowning the plant's roots.

Plant food

If you dig plenty of organic matter, such as well-rotted manure, into the soil, this should give your plants enough nourishment. However, the food provided by the potting mix in pots is soon used up. You can buy plant food, but you could also have a go at making your own.

Nettles are a great source of nutrients for plants. If the nettles are carefully cut—wear protective gloves—they can be put in a plastic bucket of water and weighed down with a brick or stone. After about six weeks, you will be able to pour off a great mixture called nettle-leaf tea, which you then dilute with water (this means mixing one part of the nettle tea with ten parts water) and use as a weekly health drink for plants that are growing in pots.

useful tools and clothes

Children thoroughly enjoy dressing up and always want to have the right tools for the job. You can indulge them in their new-found hobby by letting them use old clothes for gardening and investing in good-quality tools.

Garden tools

Kids love to have their own tools and there is a whole range out there designed to appeal to the mini-gardener. Be warned, though, as many have about the same durability and suitability for the job as a pat of butter. Before you buy, make sure that the tools have the strength to tackle soil and, remember, sometimes small adult hand tools can be better than those ostensibly aimed at kids, even though they might not look as cute.

Gardening gloves

These can be useful, but if you wash hands after every activity and don't have a child who has a "ugh" reaction to a bit of soil, they're not strictly necessary. If you do want to use gloves, get a couple of pairs so that some can be washing and drying while the others are in use.

Garden clothes

My kids have tomato-ketchup magnetism; wherever it is, it somehow lands on them. However, in this house, stained clothes become gardening clothes, and no activity is begun without donning some of these, and I would urge you to follow suit.

You can also adapt an adult shirt for this purpose (preferably one no longer in use) by cutting off the collar, shortening the arms, and adding some elastic to the ends of the sleeves. If you button this up from behind, you'll find you have a great "messy activity top," and your children will also look like little French Impressionist painters, which is a boon.

Remember also to get a pair of rain boots for your children to wear when they are working on projects outdoors.

CHAPTER 1

Windowsill Gardening

sprouting birthday cards

Why not give your friends and family birthday cards with a difference? Sticking on seeds in the shape of their initials, or perhaps their age, makes a lovely greeting that they can also grow and then eat. It will make their birthday last much longer!

① To make your template, take the piece of card and cut it in half widthwise. Decide on the shape, number, or letter that you want to create and draw this on the card. Make sure that you leave a space around the edges and try to make your design nice and bold.

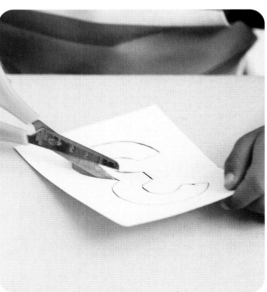

② Cut out the shape carefully with scissors. You can make a hole to start cutting by pushing a sharp pencil through the card into a ball of modeling clay. If the shape, letter, or number has a middle section, remember to leave some card to attach to this so that the template is all in one piece.

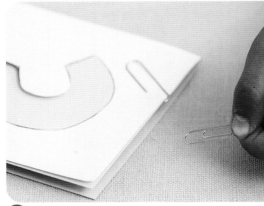

3 Take your piece of colored card and fold it in half widthwise. Write your birthday message inside. Don't forget to write the instructions for growing your seeds as well. Why not write something like this: "You can grow this card. Just put it in a shallow dish, cover it with a little potting mix, and give it some water. In a few days, you will have some lovely cress to add to your sandwiches."

4 When you have written the intriguing greeting in your card, use paper clips to attach the template to the front of it.

5 Mix together a tablespoon of sugar and a tablespoon of flour in a plastic bowl. Slowly pour in a little water from the pitcher, a few drips at a time, and mix together with the paintbrush until you have a smooth paste.

6 Carefully paint the sugar-and-flour paste onto the letter or number shape with the paintbrush. Try to apply the paste to the card as neatly and evenly as you can.

Try this... As well as cress seeds, you can also use other small seeds, such as cilantro (coriander), dill, or radish, which can be harvested as delicious microleaves.

⑦ Take your cress seeds and sprinkle them over the paste until you have completely covered the shape. You can collect any fallen seeds and sprinkle them on again if they don't stick very well at first.

⑧ Leave the paste to dry and then take off the paper clips and template. You can now put your card in its envelope ready for the lucky recipient.

christmas grass head elf

Try growing some of your Christmas decorations one year by using a little grass seed to give this cute elf some festive green hair. If you want to create a whole family of Santa's little helpers, just cut some other tubes slightly smaller to make junior elves.

③ Using the template on pages 124–5, cut out the elf's arms from the green paper and two gloves from the red paper to keep your elf's hands warm. Use the glue stick to fix the gloves to the elf's hands.

① Cut out a piece of the green paper so that it is the same height as the toilet roll inner tube and wide enough to wrap around it. Glue the piece of paper to the tube using the glue stick.

② To make the elf's smart pants, cut out a piece of the red paper so that it is half the height of the inner tube. Glue the red pants to the tube with the glue stick. Cut out a strip of black paper to make the belt and glue this around the elf's tummy where the pieces of red and green paper join.

④ Attach the arms to the tube with the glue stick. Use the black pen to draw on some buttons and to add a line to form the elf's pants.

Try this... You could use other small seeds, such as mustard or cress, to make different hairstyles for your little elves.

5 Using the template on pages 124–5, cut out the shape of the elf's face from the white paper and carefully draw on his features with the black pen. When you are happy with the elf's face, put a little glue on the back and stick it carefully to the tube.

6 Using the template on pages 124–5, cut out the elf's feet from the green card, fold the template so that the elf's feet will sit flat, and then stick the top section to the inside of the tube using the sticky tape.

7 You will want your Christmas elf to look as smart as possible, so give him a decorative belt buckle by sticking on the red pompom with the white (PVA) glue.

8 Put some absorbent cotton (cotton wool) in the yogurt pot until it nearly reaches the rim, firming it down as you go, and then dampen it with some water.

9 Carefully sprinkle some grass seed over the top of the absorbent cotton (cotton wool) . You only need to add enough to cover the surface.

10 Slide the yogurt pot into the top of the tube and leave your elf on a sunny windowsill. Make sure the absorbent cotton (cotton wool) stays damp and the green hair will begin to grow in a few days.

cress caterpillar

This caterpillar will look really great on your windowsill and, even better, it will grow delicious cress that you can snip off and add to salads or sandwiches. You can play around with the color and size of your caterpillar by using half a longer egg box or selecting different colored paints, food dyes, and pipe cleaners.

① Cut an egg box base in half lengthwise and then trim down the sides. Paint one half green with the poster paint and leave it to dry. This will be your caterpillar's body.

② Fill the bowl with water, add a few drops of the green food coloring, and drop in the three eggshell halves. Leave these for 30 minutes to dye, then take them out and let them dry on some paper towels.

③ Put a ball of modeling clay inside the egg box and then, using the pencil, poke holes into the clay through the sides. Move the clay along as you go until you have made three holes on each side for the caterpillar's legs and two at the front for the antennae.

You will need

scissors

1 egg box (half-dozen size)

green poster paint

paintbrush

small bowl

green food coloring

3 eggshell halves

paper towel

modeling clay

sharp pencil

3 green pipe cleaners

1 black pipe cleaner

pair of googly eyes

white (PVA) glue

absorbent cotton (cotton wool)

cress seeds

small plate

4 Thread the three green pipe cleaners through from one side to the other so that the legs on each side are of the same length, and then bend them downward.

Tip... Keep a small pitcher of water by the caterpillar and add a little to the eggshells every day to ensure that the absorbent cotton does not dry out.

Try this... You could also have a go at growing mustard seeds in your caterpillar instead.

5 Thread the black pipe cleaner through both holes in the front of the egg box so that the antennae are the same length, and then bend them upward. Glue the googly eyes onto the front of the caterpillar.

6 Put the dried eggshell halves into the spaces along the caterpillar's back and fill each one with a ball of absorbent cotton (cotton wool) that you have dampened in a bowl of clean water.

7 Empty some cress seeds onto a small plate and, once all of the damp absorbent cotton (cotton wool) balls are in place, carefully sprinkle the seeds on top of the balls.

You should see the cress seeds germinating within a day and your crop of little cress plants will be ready to cut and eat within 3–5 days.

microleaves farm

Many vegetables, herbs, and salads can be eaten at seedling stage when they are only "microleaves." Not only is this a very speedy way to harvest your vegetables, but it is also a good opportunity to try new bite-sized tastes. Try growing some microleaves in this tiny farm. If you can't find an old wine presentation box, then ask a grown-up to help you find one in a store.

②Once the box has dried, use the acrylic paint pens to add flower details to the front of the box. We have drawn daisies here, but you can draw whatever type of flower you like.

①Ask a grown-up to drill some drainage holes in the bottom of the wine box and remove the sliding lid. Use the paintbrush to decorate the outside and top of the box with the green poster paint. (Do not paint the base because this won't be seen.)

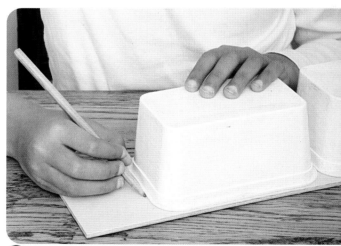

③Place two margarine tubs upside down on top of the wine-box lid and mark the gap between the two. Either ask a grown-up to cut out this section for you or use the lid as a template to cut the same shape out of thick card. Paint this section green to match the box.

You will need

wooden wine box with a sliding lid (single-bottle size)

paintbrush

green poster paint

white and yellow acrylic paint pens

2 old margarine tubs (18oz/500g capacity)

thick card (optional)

scissors

16–18 Popsicle (lollipop) sticks

white (PVA) glue

pen

thin card

colored pencils

glue stick

sharp pencil or skewer

modeling clay

gravel

seed potting mix

selection of seeds, such as radishes, cilantro (coriander), dill, beets (beetroot), arugula (rocket), or Swiss chard

a few stones

Try this... Harvest the microleaves when they are an inch or so high and have a pair of seed leaves. Snip these off using small, round-ended scissors, and give them a rinse in clean water before eating.

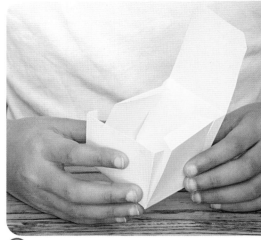

④ To make the fencing in front of the farmhouse, position one of the sticks so that it is sitting horizontally under five other sticks and then glue in place using the white (PVA) glue. Do the same for the second piece of fencing.

⑤ Using the template on pages 124–5 to help you, draw and cut out a farmhouse and its roof from a piece of thin card. Decorate the front of the farmhouse with a door and some windows using the pen and colored pencils.

⑥ To make the farmhouse walls, fold in the sections and use the glue stick on the tabs to join the sides together and form a cube. You might want to ask a grown-up to help you with this stage because it can be a bit tricky.

⑦ Color in the roof section in the same way as you did the rest of the farmhouse. Here, we have given the farmhouse a thatched roof, but you could also draw on roof tiles or slates. Stick the roof section onto the farmhouse using the white (PVA) glue.

8 Make holes in the base of the margarine tubs by carefully pushing through a sharp pencil or skewer into a ball of modeling clay. Ask a grown-up to do this if you find it difficult. Put a thick layer of gravel in the base of each tub.

9 Fill the tubs with seed potting mix, firm this down, and then sow with lines of seeds. Write the name of the seed that you've sown on a stick plant label and insert one at the end of each row.

 Try this... You might also want to decorate your farm with some toy animals to make a fun display area.

10 Add a few stones to the bottom of the wine box and then slide the top cut-out section back into position in the middle. This will form a support for the farmhouse. Slot the margarine tubs into the box so that they are sitting on either side of the support.

11 Sit the farmhouse on top of the central support and carefully push the fencing into the tubs. Place the farm on a bright sunny windowsill, remembering to water the plants regularly.

stop-motion bean pot

Ever wondered what happens to the seeds that you plant in the ground? Now you can find out with these colorful stop-motion bean pots. They will show you the stages of germination and you will be rewarded with a bean plant ready to put in the garden.

You will need

newspaper

toilet roll inner tube

sticky tape

potting mix

clear plastic pint-sized beaker

colored paper napkins

runner or green bean seeds (we used *Phaseolus coccineus* 'Celebration')

small pitcher

hand trowel, bamboo cane, pitcher, and garden twine or string (if you want to plant your beans outside)

(1) Wrap a piece of newspaper around the toilet roll inner tube, so that one end is tightly sealed up, and then secure the newspaper in place with some sticky tape.

(2) Carefully fill the inner tube with some potting mix, making sure that you firm it down inside the tube as you go. Smaller fingers are much better for this job than grown-up ones.

(3) Place the inner tube in the plastic beaker and use paper napkins to fill the space between the tube and the sides of the beaker.

Try this... Wait until the germinated beans have two true leaves and then plant them out while still on their napkins. The bits of napkin will simply rot down in the soil.

Try this... When the central bean has grown two large leaves and you are certain that there will be no more frosts, take it carefully from the beaker, dig a hole in the garden with a hand trowel, and plant it in a warm, sunny spot. Remember to water it in well. Support the bean plant by tying it to a bamboo cane using garden twine or string in a figure-of-eight pattern.

④ Using your index finger, make a hole about 1½in (4cm) deep in the potting mix. You can use a pen or pencil to do this instead, but it's not as much fun as using your finger.

⑤ Plant a bean seed in the hole, cover it over with more potting mix, and then firm down. Try not to spill any potting mix over the side of the tube or you won't be able to see your beans grow later.

⑥ Push another bean seed approximately 1½in (4cm) down the side of the beaker, making sure that you are able to see it clearly from the outside.

(7) With a small pitcher, slowly add water to the tube and beaker so that the potting mix and napkins are both damp. Every two days, push another bean down the side of the beaker but a little further along, and make sure that the napkins do not dry out.

Watch the beans begin to germinate one by one and then, as you turn the beaker around, you will be able to see the whole germination process unfold from start to finish.

Try this... you can also grow climbing green beans or a dwarf runner bean variety.

mini window box salad garden

You don't need lots of space to grow tasty salad leaves. Using old wooden wine containers, you can create pint-sized window boxes that will give you delicious leaves for weeks on end. Just remember, there is not a lot of potting mix in these boxes, so make sure that you water them every day to stop them drying out.

You will need

wooden wine box (single-bottle size)	paint dish
paintbrush	red wood stain
cream wood stain	fine-tipped paintbrush
1 large potato	black acrylic paint
sharp knife	gravel
black pen or 2 cookie cutters (one in the shape of a leaf and one in the shape of a rabbit's head)	seed potting mix
	cut-and-come-again lettuce seeds
green wood stain	watering can with a fine rose

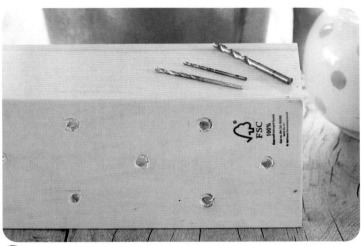

① Ask a grown-up to drill some drainage holes in the base of the wine box. These holes are important because they will allow excess water to drain away.

② Paint the wine box all over (apart from the base) with cream wood stain. After it has dried, apply a second coat. Once the second coat has dried thoroughly, turn the box over and paint the base with two coats (also allowing them to dry between applications).

③ To make the printers, cut the potato in half, draw the rabbit's head on one half and the leaf shape on the other with a black pen, and ask a grown-up to cut around the shapes carefully with the knife. Alternatively, use cookie cutters to press a leaf shape in one half of the potato and a rabbit's-head shape in the other half. If the grown-up then cuts away the potato up to the shapes with the sharp knife, you are left with your two potato printers.

Try this... Do not throw away your lettuce thinnings. Give them a good wash and you can eat these tasty baby leaves as well.

You can ask a grown-up to attach your window box with screws and brackets to the front of your playhouse or simply place it on a window ledge.

④ Put some green wood stain in a paint dish, dip in your leaf-shape potato printer and, once it is evenly coated in wood stain, press it carefully onto the side of the box. Do this again and again until you have built up a pattern of leaves, and then allow to dry. Wash out your paint dish and put in some red wood stain when it is dry. Coat the rabbit's-head potato printer in the red wood stain and use it to add bunny heads in between the leaf shapes.

⑤ Using the fine-tipped paintbrush, carefully paint three whiskers and a pair of eyes on each side of your bunny heads using the black acrylic paint. You need a steady hand for this, so ask a grown-up for help if necessary.

Try this... You can also decorate your planted window box with toy windmills and rabbits.

6 When the wood stain is completely dry, put a layer of gravel in the base of the box and fill to just below the top with the potting mix, pressing down firmly.

7 Thinly sow a mix of cut-and-come-again lettuce seeds on the surface of the potting mix and water them in using a watering can with a fine rose.

8 As they grow, gradually thin out your seedlings by removing the smaller ones and leaving the stronger ones. Make sure that there is a space of about 2½–4in (5–10cm) between each one. Pull off the lettuce leaves regularly, leaving in the roots and base of the plant, and new leaves will grow to replace them.

budding bunny ears

The cut-off ends of carrots can carry on growing fresh leaves. Just keep them well watered in a sunny spot and you'll have sprouting bunny ears in a week or two. You can even plant your sprouted carrot tops in the garden. They will eventually form little flowers and later seeds, which you can collect and sow to grow, you guessed it, more carrots!

You will need

small plastic water bottle

sandpaper

paintbrush

water-based acrylic or eggshell paint (in any color your like)

scissors

pieces of black and white felt

white (PVA) glue

pompom

googly eyes

string

sand

1 carrot

small pitcher

① Ask a grown-up to cut the top off a small plastic water bottle (make sure that you keep both parts as well as the screw-top lid). Use a piece of sandpaper to rub all over the bottle. This will help the paint stick to the plastic surface.

② Paint the outside of both the top and bottom of the bottle with the water-based acrylic or eggshell paint in the color you would like your rabbit to be. You may need to apply two or three coats (allowing each coat to dry in between) to achieve a good solid color.

③ When the paint has dried, cut out the shapes for the rabbit's eyes and mouth from the pieces of felt. Glue these to the bottom part of the bottle and then glue on the pompom nose in between. Don't forget to glue on the googly eyes as well.

④ Ask a grown-up to help you cut some short pieces of string for the whiskers. Roll the pieces of string in the glue, and then stick the whiskers on either side of your rabbit's mouth.

⑤ With the lid screwed on, turn the top of the bottle that you cut off earlier upside down and add a small amount of sand for the carrot top to sit on. Put the top of the bottle inside the bottom of the bottle.

⑥ Ask a grown-up to cut the top off the carrot for you. Make sure that the carrot top is about ¾in (2cm) deep. Put the carrot top on the sand, fill up this part of the bottle with water using the small pitcher, and place the finished bunny on a light windowsill. Keep the water topped up and you will see new "ears" begin to shoot within a day or two.

BUDDING BUNNY EARS

43

Vegetable & Herb Gardening

hula-hoop cloche

Building a cloche is like putting a cozy blanket over your plants. It will keep the soil warmer, which means that you can start sowing seeds earlier in the spring and keep plants growing longer into the fall and even the winter. Best of all, the colorful Hula-Hoop frame will look great all year round.

① Insert the lengths of bamboo cane into the ends of your four Hula-Hoop sections so that half of a bamboo cane is sticking out from each end of the hoops.

② Push the bamboo part of the hoop structure into the earth on either side of the crops that you need to protect or the seeds and soil that you would like to warm up.

③ Ask a grown-up or friend to help you cover the hoops with the piece of horticultural fleece. It is a much easier job if there are two of you.

 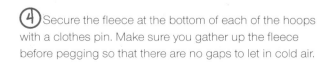 Try this...In the summer months, why not take off the horticultural fleece and use your cloche frame as a colorful support for growing dwarf climbing beans or pea plants?

④ Secure the fleece at the bottom of each of the hoops with a clothes pin. Make sure you gather up the fleece before pegging so that there are no gaps to let in cold air.

You will need

2 Hula-Hoops (ask a grown-up to cut them in half)

8 pieces of bamboo cane, 1.5ft (40cm) long

6ft (2m) length of horticultural fleece

8 large, colored clothes pins

climbing bean archway

With a few magic beans you can rival Jack and his beanstalk by creating this spectacular archway. You can watch as the bean seeds sprout and then race up to the top of the bamboo canes in just a few short weeks. Not only will your bean plants give you pretty flowers and delicious beans, but you can also use the archway to create an impressive entrance to a vegetable garden or play area.

You will need

pen and card

scissors

2 tall terracotta plant pots, at least 10in (25cm) in diameter

old newspaper

masking tape

green emulsion paint

large and small paintbrush

white acrylic paint pen

gravel or small stones

potting mix

watering can

4 bamboo canes

garden twine or string

runner or green bean seeds (we used *Phaseolus coccineus* 'Celebration')

1 Using the templates on pages 124–5, draw the bean pod and leaf shapes on two pieces of card and carefully cut them out to form your stencils.

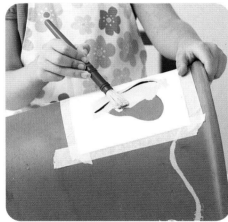

2 With your pot placed on some old newspaper, use the masking tape to position the stencil on the pot and paint over the pattern with the green emulsion paint using the large paintbrush. Allow the paint to dry and then continue to paint pods and leaves over the whole pot.

3 Use the green paint and the small paintbrush to add the stems and tendrils that link the bean leaves and pods. Add veins and other fine details with the white acrylic paint pen. Repeat steps 2 and 3 on the second pot.

Try this...You can use bamboo canes of different lengths in order to make the archway taller or shorter, depending on who will be using it.

④ When there is no danger of frost, you can plant your beans outside. Place your pots where you want the archway to be (this needs to be somewhere quite sunny) and then put some gravel or stones in the bottom of each before filling with potting mix, firming it down as you go. Water in well with the watering can.

⑤ Push two bamboo canes into each pot on opposite sides to each other.

⑥ Tie the first pair of bamboo canes together tightly at the top using twine or string and then do the same with the other pair. Tie the two pairs of canes together to form the central point of the archway.

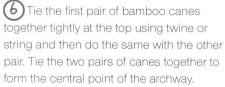

7 With your finger, make a hole in the potting mix next to one of the canes. The hole should be three times deeper than the beans are wide. Drop the bean in the hole, cover over, and firm down. Do this again on the other side of the cane, so that you will have two bean plants for each cane. Repeat for the other three uprights.

8 To help the plants start climbing, gently tie in the stems to the canes using twine or string in a figure-of-eight knot. This will stop the stems rubbing on the cane and damaging the plant. As the bean plants grow, they will climb the canes until they reach the top, creating a leafy archway.

Try this... Pick the beans regularly when they start to appear because this encourages the plant to produce more.

mini scarecrow

Full-size scarecrows can look a little out of place in a small vegetable patch. Use some old children's clothes and you can create a cuter, cut-down version. If you don't have a little brother, sister, or cousin who has grown out of some clothes for dressing your scarecrow, have a look in local thrift stores (charity shops) to see what you can find.

You will need

thick bamboo cane, approximately 20in (50cm) long

old broomstick

garden twine or string

long-sleeved child's T-shirt

small children's dungarees

old plastic bags, scrunched-up newspaper, or straw

small amount of straw

terracotta plant pot, approximately 8in (20cm) in diameter (with a small or no drainage hole)

old straw hat

① Put the bamboo cane across the broom handle about a third of the way down from the top to form a cross shape. Wrap the garden twine or string several times around the join in a figure-of-eight pattern and then tie it tightly to hold the cross shape together.

② "Dress" the cross shape in the old T-shirt and then put the pair of dungarees over the top. Tie or button up the dungarees so that they fit your scarecrow.

③ Using the twine or string, tie the ends of the sleeves and pants (trousers) closed, but leave a very small gap for adding some straw later.

Try this... Why not make scarecrows in different sizes using clothes for babies, toddlers, and children? Just make the length of the broom handles slightly smaller each time.

4 Use the old plastic bags, scrunched-up newspaper or straw to fill the body of the scarecrow, starting at the bottom of the legs and then working your way upward.

5 Push a little straw into the ends of the sleeves and pants (trousers) to form hands and feet, and more around the top of the T-shirt to look like a neck.

6 Ask a grown-up to push the base of the long broom handle into the ground in the spot you've chosen, so that the scarecrow is secure and standing just above the soil. Place the plant-pot head on the scarecrow and finish off by adding the hat.

herb-tasting tower

Planting a strawberry pot is a great way to grow lots of different herbs in a small space. You can pick the herbs whenever you need some fresh flavors to add to your favorite dishes. Try to choose herbs that you enjoy tasting and smelling, but avoid planting mint because this has a habit of taking over and so is best given a pot of its own.

1 Put a layer of large gravel or stones in the base of the strawberry pot. Add some of the potting mix until it is nearly level with the first holes in the pot.

Carefully take the first herbs out of their pots and then slip them into the holes from the outside in. Add more potting mix around the roots of the herbs and keep filling with potting mix until the next planting holes are reached. Plant more herbs in the same way.

2 Finish off by planting the chives in the large opening at the top of the pot, firming in the potting mix around the plant. Make sure that the chive plant is sitting straight because it is the centerpiece of the display. Water the strawberry pot thoroughly but gently, so that you don't wash potting mix out of the holes. Remember to use the rose attachment on the watering can. If any potting mix washes out of the holes, just push it back in.

3 Use a pen to write the name of each herb on the end of the sticks. This will help you to remember the names of the herbs later. Push each stick into the hole next to the plant. Place the pot somewhere sunny and turn it regularly so that all of the herbs get enough sun.

VEGETABLE & HERB GARDENING

54

bird scarer

Birds are great to watch in the garden but sometimes they can be tempted to eat your seeds, fruit or even young plants. Keep them away from your crops and brighten up your vegetable patch at the same time with this pretty bird scarer.

You will need

4 bamboo canes

garden twine or string

long length of thin ribbon

old CD

lengths of wider ribbon and sparkly tinsel

silver milk-bottle tops

pencil and modeling clay

① Take the bamboo canes and push two of them into the ground at either end of your row of crops to form upside-down "V"-shapes. If you find this difficult, then ask a grown-up to help you.

② Tie the bamboo canes tightly together using the garden twine or string in a figure-of-eight pattern. Again, ask your grown-up to help you tie the twine or string really tightly.

③ Measure off a piece of the thin ribbon so that it is approximately 8in (20cm) longer than the gap between the two bamboo-cane supports.

Try this... Birds will get used to your bird scarer after a few days, so why not change around some of the items on the ribbon? You could try adding strips of aluminum foil or plastic bags—anything that is shiny or moves about will scare away birds.

4 Tie one end of the ribbon to the first set of bamboo canes before threading on the old CD and then tie the other end to the second set of bamboo canes. Remember to ask a grown-up for permission to use the CD first.

5 Tie the wider ribbons and pieces of tinsel onto the central ribbon, making sure that you space these out at regular intervals. Make holes in the bottle tops by pushing the pencil through them into a ball of modeling clay. Thread the bottle tops onto some ribbons, which have been knotted at one end, and then tie them onto the string. The fluttering ribbons and tinsel will scare away any birds.

herbal bath bags

Harvested herbs from the garden aren't just for eating. You can use them, whether fresh or dry, to make scented herbal bath bags. These can be tied over the hot tap when you're ready for a super-scented soak in the tub.

You will need

large dinner plate

pencil

piece of muslin

pinking shears

fresh or dried herbs, such as lavender, sage, rosemary, thyme, mint, and bay leaves

rubber band

pretty ribbons

1 Take the plate and draw around it with the pencil on the piece of muslin. Cut out the circle of muslin with the pinking shears. Using pinking shears will stop the fabric from fraying at the edges.

Try this... You can dry herbs for your bath bags by hanging them upside down for a few weeks in small bunches somewhere warm and dry.

2 Put your chosen herbs in the middle of the circle of muslin. If you are going to use the bath bags straight away, use sprigs of fresh herbs. If you want to keep them for longer, then use dried herbs.

3 Gather together the fabric and twist it around so that the herbs are contained in the center of the piece of muslin. Use a rubber band to secure the fabric tightly.

4 Take one of the ribbons and tie it carefully over the rubber band so that the band is hidden from view. Tie a double knot so that it won't come loose and then you can tie the ribbon into a bow on top in order to finish it off.

Slip another length of ribbon under the neck of the first ribbon and the rubber band, and tie this on with a knot. Ask a grown-up to use this section of ribbon to secure your bath bag to the hot tap at bath-time.

wheelbarrow vegetable garden

You don't need acres of space, or even a garden, to grow tasty vegetables. Using an old wheelbarrow and some well-chosen seeds and plants, you can create a mobile mini vegetable plot. As the wheelbarrow isn't very deep, it is worth avoiding root vegetables or choose only very small varieties.

You will need

- old wheelbarrow
- scrubbing brush
- warm, soapy water
- gravel
- potting mix
- water-retaining granules
- garden twine or string
- clothes pins
- selection of dwarf or compact seed species or small plants, as follows:
    - 1 mini fava (broad) bean plant
    - 1 cherry tomato plant
    - beets (beetroot) seed
    - 'Tom Thumb' lettuce seeds
    - 'Parmex' carrot seeds
    - radish seeds
- short sticks or bamboo canes
- watering can with a fine rose

① Ask your grown-up to drill or puncture holes every 4–6in (10–15cm) in the base of the wheelbarrow. Use the scrubbing brush and warm, soapy water to give the wheelbarrow a good clean, and then leave it to dry. Add a layer of gravel, about ¾–1¼in (2–3cm) deep, to the bottom of the wheelbarrow to help with drainage.

② Add some potting mix to the wheelbarrow so that it comes to within 1¾–2in (4–5cm) of the top. Add some water-retaining granules and then mix them into the potting mix.

③ Use lengths of garden twine or string to mark out six square sections over the top of the wheelbarrow and to form mini fences. Use the clothes pins to secure the ends of the twine or string to the rim of the barrow.

④ Plant a different seed species or plant in each square. Place the tallest plants at the deeper end of the wheelbarrow, in order to give their roots more room to grow, and plant the smaller ones toward the front.

⑤ Plants such as tomatoes and beans may grow quite tall, so push a short stick or bamboo cane into the potting mix next to these plants so that you can tie them in as they grow taller.

⑥ Water the plants thoroughly, using the fine rose on the end of your watering can so that you don't disturb the potting mix around the seeds. Keep the barrow well watered and then harvest your vegetables when they reach maturity.

Simple Crafts

pine cone bird feeder

Bird feeders don't have to be boring. Using some bright fall berries and sparkling pine cones will give the birds a treat, as well as create an eye-catching decoration for your garden. Make sure you hang the feeder near to a window so that you can watch the birds feeding.

① Using your paintbrush, carefully apply the gold or silver paint to the scales of the smaller pine cones, and then leave them to dry.

② Tie one end of the string or twine around the center of the largest pine cone and then tie the small pine cones and sprays of rowan berries at intervals along its length, leaving at least 8in (20cm) clear at the end.

③ Put the birdseed, flour, oatmeal, and white fat (lard) in the mixing bowl. Mix all the bird-food ingredients together using your hands. Although it is easier this way (and also more fun), wear an apron because you may get messy in the process.

Try this... Once you start feeding garden birds, keep doing so, as they will come to rely on these snacks. If you want to make decorative feeders in the winter, you could collect a lot of berries and ask a grown-up to freeze them for you.

You will need

paintbrush

gold or silver acrylic paint

paint tray or plastic container

2–3 small pine cones

garden twine or string, 24in (60cm) in length

1 large pine cone

rowan berries (you could also use hawthorn berries or rosehips)

½ cup (65g) birdseed

½ cup (65g) flour

1 cup (125g) oatmeal

½ cup (115g) white fat (lard), at room temperature

mixing bowl

apron

4 Push the mixture into the gaps in the large pine cone until it is as full as possible. When you have finished, ask a grown-up to hang your bird feeder in a tree or somewhere you can easily watch your feathered friends come and visit.

ice mobiles

When temperatures drop you can still add some life to your garden with these beautiful ice mobiles. Hang them from bare branches to brighten up your backyard and, remember, the colder it is, the longer they will last.

You will need

plain or shaped silicone cupcake molds

large flat-bottomed plastic container

selection of fall berries, such as sorbus, pyracantha or cotoneaster

sparkly glitter

pretty ribbon

small jug

Try this.. .You can use other natural decorative items from the garden instead of the berries. Why not try freezing some tiny pebbles, seedheads, or leaves with the glitter?

① Place the cupcake molds in a row in the plastic container and add some fall berries to each mold. Here, we have used sorbus berries, but you can use any type of brightly colored berries that you like.

② Carefully sprinkle a little of the sparkly glitter into each of the molds. Try to get a nice mixture of colors because then the glitter will really catch the light when you hang the mobile outside.

3 Place the length of ribbon across all the molds so that it dangles into each one and there is at least 12in (30cm) spare at one end. Carefully pour water from the jug into each of the molds until they are all full.

4 Ask a grown-up to put the container in a freezer overnight and, when it is frozen, push the ice shape out of each mold. Your ice mobile can now be hung on a branch in the garden.

scented flower soaps

Use pressed flowers to make pretty scented soaps. These make lovely gifts and are perfect for treating yourself. Washing your hands has never been such fun. You can usually find glycerine soap and essential oils in health food stores or pharmacies.

You will need

small flowers or leaves

sheets of letter size (A4) paper

sheets of newspaper

heavy books

ice cube tray

4oz (115g) glycerine soap

plastic pitcher

plastic wrap

essential oil, such as lavender oil

Try this... You can use different-colored flowers to make a rainbow-themed set of soaps.

① Pick some pretty flowers or leaves from your garden (smaller ones work best). Remember to ask a grown-up for permission to do this first. Place them between sheets of paper backed by sheets of newspaper. Put all these sheets between some heavy books. It will take around two weeks for the flowers to be fully pressed and dried.

② Put one or two pressed flowers in each compartment of your empty ice cube tray. Ask a grown-up to cut the bar of glycerine soap into three, place the pieces in a plastic pitcher covered with plastic wrap, and then heat in a microwave on full power for 20-second intervals until it has all melted. If you haven't got a microwave, ask your grown-up helper to melt the soap in a saucepan over a low heat on the stove-top.

③ Carefully add three or four drops of your favorite essential oil to the melted soap (lavender is a good one to use because it smells lovely and is relaxing, too).

④ Ask an adult to pour the melted soap gently into the ice cube tray on top of the flowers. Make sure that the flowers are still sitting centrally in each compartment. Put the soaps in the fridge to set.

⑤ After about 30 minutes, the soaps should have set and you can remove from the refrigerator and carefully press them out of the ice cube tray.

pressed flower placemats

Do you wish flowers would last for longer? Well, why not enjoy them all year round by making these useful placemats? You could even press flowers at different times of the year to create a range of placemats for every season.

You will need

- small flowers
- sheets of letter size (A4) paper
- sheets of newspaper
- heavy books
- large plate
- pencil
- thick card
- scissors
- contact paper or sticky-backed plastic
- white (PVA) glue

1. Pick some small flowers from your favorite garden plants, remembering to ask a grown-up for permission first. Making sure the flowers aren't touching each other, place them between sheets of paper followed by sheets of newspaper before pressing them between heavy books. You will need to leave them for two weeks so that they are fully dry.

2. Draw around the large plate with the pencil to make a circle on the piece of thick card. Cut out the circle carefully using scissors. Also draw a round circle of contact paper or sticky-backed plastic using the same plate, and cut out.

 Try this... You can make matching coasters by drawing around a large mug or small bowl to create a smaller circle.

③ Arrange the flowers on your card circle and, when you are happy with the pattern, stick them on carefully by putting a small dab of white (PVA) glue onto the back of each flower.

④ When your pattern is finished and the glue has dried, peel away a section of the contact paper, position it carefully over the mat, and press down. Then, start to peel away the rest of the backing, smoothing down the contact paper as you go.

fall leaf picture frame

Fall leaves are far too gorgeous to be just trodden under foot. How about saving some of your favourite leaf specimens to create this lovely seasonal picture frame instead?

You will need

plastic bowl

felt-tip pen

large paper plate

scissors

card

sharp pencil and modeling clay

4 split pins and string

selection of leaves

white (PVA) glue

2 large plates

coloring pencils

1 Draw around the plastic bowl with the pen to create a circle in the center of the large paper plate. Use scissors to carefully cut out the central circle.

2 Cut out three leaf-shaped retainers from a piece of card and make holes in the bottom of each leaf by pushing through the sharp pencil into a ball of modeling clay to stop it damaging the table. In the same way, make three holes around the inside edge of the picture frame.

3 Push a split pin through each of the retainers and the paper plate, and open out the pin on the front side of the frame.

④ Using the pencil and modeling clay, make another two holes at the top of the frame and thread through a piece of string before tying it to form a picture hanger.

⑤ Use white (PVA) glue to stick your selection of leaves to the front of the plate frame.

Try this... You can put a thin coat of white (pva) glue over all of the leaves on the frame to make them nice and shiny. This will also help stop the leaves crumbling as they dry.

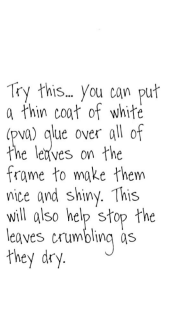

⑥ To make sure it bonds well, sandwich the picture frame between two large plates, weigh down with something heavy, and leave to dry for an hour.

7 Draw a circle on a piece of card which is just larger than the hole in the frame and draw your picture for framing on this card. Then, slide the finished picture under the leaf retainers to hold it in place.

jam jar garden lights

With some beads, pens, sand, and a tea-light, you can turn a boring old jam jar into a pretty night-light for the garden. If you use a citronella candle, you will even find it helps to ward off mosquitoes and other biting insects.

You will need

old jam jar

acrylic paint pens

thin garden wire, 20in (50cm) long

glass, porcelain, or plastic beads

play sand

plastic container or glass jar with a lid

food coloring

citronella tea-light

①Decorate your old jar using the acrylic paint pens, and then leave it to dry. Here, we have decorated the jar with lots of pretty flowers, but you can paint on any design that you like.

②Put a loop at one end of the wire and thread on the beads from the other end until half the wire is covered (the loop will stop the beads from slipping off).

③Wrap the unbeaded part of the wire around the neck of the jam jar, twisting the end to secure it. Bend the beaded section over to form a handle, leaving a little clear wire at the end. Hook this under the neck wire and then twist it to keep the handle securely in place.

Tip... Remember, never light the candle yourself. Always ask an adult to help you and only have the candle lit when there is a grown-up with you.

④ Put two or three handfuls of play sand into the bottom of another container or jar. Add a few drops of the food coloring to the sand. Put the lid on tightly and shake the container or jar hard for 30 seconds.

⑤ Pour the colored sand into the bottom of the decorated jam jar and then gently drop the citronella tea-light on top of the sand for lighting later on.

insect hotel

Give your local mini beasts somewhere to shelter and hide in style with this multi-story insect hotel. You'll find it soon fills up with lots of garden visitors, from bees and ladybugs to lacewings and woodlice.

You will need

24 old bricks

old curved roof tiles

10 short pieces of wood

materials to fill the hotel, such as corrugated cardboard, bamboo canes, drinking straws, old pots, logs, egg boxes, pine cones, and dry leaves

a selection of hollow tubes (including empty cardboard tubes and plastic pipes or bottles)

① Find a quiet, sheltered spot in the garden and make sure that the ground is flat. Put down two rows of bricks, two bricks long and two bricks high, so that they are the same width apart as the length of your pieces of wood.

② Put a curved roof tile between the two rows of bricks to provide a shelter for toads and frogs. Lay three pieces of wood, spaced at equal distances, across the lines of bricks. Add another one or two courses of bricks and some more wood in order to build up the stories.

③ On the top layer, add an extra piece of wood at the back of the stack. This will make the tiles sit at an angle, which will help the rain run off.

④ Roll up pieces of corrugated cardboard so that you can slide them inside the old cardboard tubes. Put the filled tubes inside the hotel and then fill the other cardboard tubes and plastic pipes with a selection of hollows stems such as sections of bamboo and drinking straws. These make perfect winter "rooms" for small insects.

(5) Why not ask an adult to drill holes in the ends of logs to include in your hotel? You can also add other materials like old egg boxes, pine cones, and dry leaves. Place more tiles on top of the final layer to form the roof of the hotel.

Try this... Why not find a flat tile or piece of slate and write the name of your hotel on it with chalk or acrylic paint pens?

ice bowl

If you want to have a really special tea outside, this is a great way to impress your friends and family. Choose your favorite leaves or flowers and create a spectacular ice bowl. Not only is this bowl a lovely way in which to serve fruit, but it will also keep it perfectly chilled.

You will need

2 plastic bowls, one slightly larger than the other

small pitcher

selection of flowers or leaves

towel

large stones

sticky tack

crêpe bandages

aluminum foil

① Take the larger of the two plastic bowls and fill it with water using the pitcher to a depth of about 5in (2cm). Ask a grown-up to put the bowl in the freezer for a few hours until the water has frozen solid.

Try this... When you put your beautiful ice bowl on display outside, put it on a tray or deep plate to collect the water as it gradually melts.

② Take the bowl out of the freezer when the water has frozen. Start wetting your chosen flowers or leaves and then place them around the inside of the bowl. The wetness will help them to stick to the sides.

③ When you have added your selection of flowers or leaves, put the second bowl inside the first one and place both on top of a towel (this will help mop up any spillages).

④ Put the large stones in the smaller bowl. This will help to keep the small bowl weighed down as the water freezes.

⑤ Take four equally sized lumps of sticky tack and place them around the edge of the larger bowl at even intervals. Mold them over the top of the rim so that they stay in place and act as buffers to hold the smaller bowl at an equal distance on all sides.

⑥ Take two lengths of crêpe bandage. Place the first under the two bowls and tie it as tightly as possible on the top. Do the same with the second bandage at right angles to the first.

7 Pour in water using your small pitcher to fill up the gap between the two plastic bowls. Keep pouring carefully until the water level nearly reaches the top.

8 Ask your grown-up to put the bowls back in the freezer carefully. You will have to be patient now and leave your ice bowl to freeze overnight.

Next day, ask your grown-up to take the bowls out of the freezer. Stand them on the towel and leave them for a few minutes until you are able to loosen the bowls.

Carefully untie the bandages and take out your finished ice bowl. If you are not using the bowl straight away, then you can store it in the freezer wrapped in aluminum foil.

Growing Projects

You will need

piece of string, 20in (50cm) in length

tent peg

plastic water bottle

play sand

special bulb planter

crocus bulbs

fairy rings

Add some magic to your lawn in the spring by planting crocus bulbs to create your very own fairy rings. Even if no fairies appear, the rings are still a great place for having a picnic and playing. Best of all, the flowers will appear again every spring.

② Ask a grown-up to use the bulb planter to make a hole along this circle every 4in (10cm) and leave the "plug" of soil and grass by the side of the hole. The hole should only be about 2in (5cm) below the surface of the grass.

① In late fall, tie one end of the piece of string to the tent peg and push this into your chosen area of lawn. Fill the plastic bottle with some play sand and tie the other end of the string to its neck. Carefully tip out a line of sand as you move the string around in a circle, keeping it taut all the time. This will mark out your fairy ring.

③ Place a crocus bulb in each hole, making sure that the bulb is the right way up (the pointed end should be facing upward). Replace the plug of soil and turf, and firm it down well. The bulbs will grow through the grass the following spring.

Try this... Make sure that the crocus ring section of the lawn is not cut until about six weeks after the flowers have finished. This gives the plant a chance to put the energy from its old leaves back into the bulb ready to grow again next year.

rainbow cutting garden

This small cutting garden will give you weeks of flowers in spring, so that you can create colorful bouquets to decorate the house or give to friends. Because you are cutting the flowers, the bulbs will not have the energy to produce further blooms the following year. This means that you will need to replant the garden again in the fall if you want to create another flowering rainbow.

You will need

garden fork

rake

piece of string, at least 39in (1m) in length

tent peg

scissors

felt-tip pen

measuring tape

cockleshells

a selection of spring bulbs, as follows: tulips, e.g. *Tulipa* 'Oscar' and 'Brilliant Star' (red), T. 'Little Princess' and 'Ballerina' (orange), T. 'Westpoint' (yellow), T. 'Blue Ribbon', and T. 'Purple Prince'; daffodils, e.g *Narcissus* 'February Gold'; grape hyacinths, e.g. *Muscari armeniacum* (blue); and blue hyacinths, e.g. *Hyacinthus* 'Blue Jacket'

small spade or special bulb planter

① Choose a sunny spot in the garden and fork over a patch of ground, about 36in (90cm) deep by 6ft (2m) wide. Remove any large stones and weeds, and rake it level. Tie the end of the piece of string to the tent peg, measure a 36in (90cm) length, and cut. Using a felt-tip pen and a measuring tape, mark the string clearly at 8in (20cm) intervals. Push the tent peg into the soil at the bottom center-point of the garden. Holding the other end of the string, move it slowly around, placing cockleshells in a line as you go to mark the first arc of the rainbow.

② Repeat this procedure for every mark on the piece of string, remembering to keep the piece of string taut at all times, until you have five arcs made from the pretty cockleshells.

③ Place the different-colored flower bulbs in the arc of that color, starting with red tulips in the first arc, then orange tulips, yellow daffodils and tulips, blue muscari and hyacinths, and purple tulips. Leave a 2in (5cm) space between the smallest bulbs and a 4in (10cm) between the larger ones.

4 Using the small spade or bulb planter, plant each bulb at three times its own depth, cover with soil, and firm down. In spring, you can cut your rainbow flowers and use them to make colorful flower arrangements for indoors.

Try this... When you have cut all the spring flowers, reuse the space to plant a rainbow of summer annuals for cutting. For example, try growing red mimulus, yellow and orange African and French marigolds (Tagetes), orange zinnias, yellow pansies (Viola x wittrockiana), and blue and purple petunias or pansies.

lawn names

If you use old cardboard boxes to make giant letters, you can write your name on the lawn or even make huge patterns. You could also create a birthday greeting ready for an outdoor party.

You will need

pen

old cardboard boxes

scissors

large stones

① Draw the letters of your name on large pieces of cardboard box (you can write your first and second names if you wish). You will need to write each letter on a different piece of cardboard and make sure your letters are very big and chunky.

② Cut out the letters carefully with the scissors. If you think that you won't be able to do this neatly enough, then just ask your grown-up for some help.

③ Position your selection of letters on a freshly mown lawn and then weigh them down with large stones so that they don't blow away in the wind.

④ Leave the letters in place for around 5–7 days. You can lift them up to check if the grass beneath is yellowing. When you can see a color difference, remove the stones and cards, and you will be able to see your name written in the grass.

Tip...Ask whoever is mowing the lawn to wait until you can see a color change in the grass. That way, you will be able to replace the letters and stones after the lawn is cut.

scented hopscotch

Thymes are very accommodating plants. Not only will they let you stand on them, they will even smell delicious while you're doing it. This makes them perfect for planting as part of a sweet-smelling game of garden hopscotch.

You will need

pieces of white card

ruler and pencil or a computer, sheets of letter size (A4) paper and tracing paper

scissors

10 small paving slabs, approximately 12 x 12in (30 x 30cm)

white masonry paint

paintbrush

horticultural grit or very small stones

garden fork

rake

small spade

16 small thyme (*Thymus*) plants

decorative gravel

Try this... If you land on one of the thyme plants as you hop from number to number, you'll find that this releases their delicious scent into the air.

① Draw the numbers 1 to 10 on the pieces of card using the ruler and pencil. Alternatively, you can use a computer to print out ten large numbers and then use tracing paper to transfer the numbers onto the pieces of card.

② Using scissors, carefully cut out each of the numbers to form your number stencils. Ask a grown-up to help you get started if you find it difficult to make your first cut in the card.

③ Place the number "1" stencil over the center of the first paving slab and, holding it carefully with one hand, use the other to apply masonry paint over the number with the paintbrush. Carefully remove the stencil and leave the slab to dry. Do the same for all the numbers up to "10."

④ Choose a piece of ground that is sunny for most of the day. Thyme plants like well-drained soil, so, unless you have this sort of soil, it is worth digging in plenty of horticultural grit or very small stones using a garden fork to improve the drainage.

⑤ When the soil is prepared, use a rake to remove about 2in (5cm) of soil from the hopscotch area and then make sure the ground is flat and free of large stones and weeds.

Try this... Why not add some lavender plants around the edge of your hopscotch area in order to make it even more scented?

⑥ Set out the ten small paving slabs in order to make a hopscotch pattern, leaving a 2–4in (5–10cm) gap between each one. These are the spaces in which you'll eventually plant your thyme plants.

⑦ Using the rake, pull the soil back over to fill in the gaps and the area around the slabs so that the slabs are sitting just above the level of the soil, but their base is buried.

⑧ Using the small spade or even your hands, dig some holes between the paving slabs for the small thyme plants. Plant some thyme plants between the paving slabs and some around the edge of the hopscotch run.

⑨ Firm in the soil around the thyme plants and then finish off your scented hopscotch site by sprinkling the decorative gravel around the plants. This will also help to keep moisture in the soil. Water everything in well and keep watering the thyme plants regularly until they are growing happily. Remember that the best time to water plants is early in the morning or in the evening.

tyrannosaurus garden

Ferns have been growing for millions of years. In fact, they are as old as the dinosaurs themselves! Use them alongside "rock" mountains and "moss" floors to create your very own prehistoric landscape in a cleverly decorated old tire.

You will need

- old car tire
- warm, soapy water
- orange acrylic paint
- paint dish
- small paint roller or piece of sponge
- old potting-mix bag
- scissors
- garden fork
- potting mix
- 2–3 fern plants or other small foliage plants, such as holly ferns (*Crytomium falcatum*), Polypody fern (*Polypodium vulgare*), and *Heuchera* 'Beauty Color'
- watering can
- 2–3 large rocks or pebbles
- moss (real or sisal)
- selection of small plastic dinosaurs
- small paintbrush

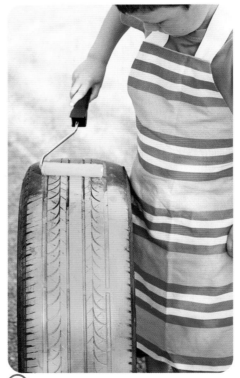

1 Give your tire a good wash with some warm, soapy water and allow it dry. Put some orange acrylic paint in the paint dish and use the paint roller or small piece of sponge to apply it around the outside of the tire. You will need to add a few coats to build up the color, allowing the paint to dry in between each coat.

2 Find a nice shady spot for your old tire (ferns don't like to be planted in the sun). Take an old potting-mix bag and cut out a section that is large enough to cover the base of the tire and a little way up the side.

(3) Place the section of potting-mix bag in the bottom of the tire and use a garden fork to puncture some holes in it. You may want to ask your grown-up to help you with this. Putting holes in the plastic will allow water to drain slowly from the tire, keeping the soil quite moist but not soaking wet.

(4) Fill the tire with some potting mix, making sure that you push it right into the inside ring of the tire as well as the center. When your tire is half full, take the plants carefully out of their pots and place them around the tire until you are happy with the layout.

(5) Fill the remaining space in the tire with some more of the potting mix, firming it down as you go along, and then water the plants in well.

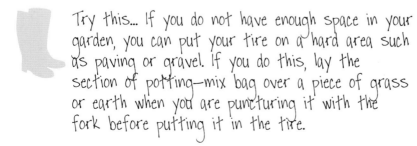

Try this... If you do not have enough space in your garden, you can put your tire on a hard area such as paving or gravel. If you do this, lay the section of potting-mix bag over a piece of grass or earth when you are puncturing it with the fork before putting it in the tire.

6 Arrange the rocks or pebbles in your prehistoric world, cover any areas of potting mix that are showing with some moss, and then introduce your dinosaurs to their new home. Use the small paintbrush to add some rivers of orange volcanic larva to one of the stones.

sunflower alley

Gigantic sunflowers are great to look at, but even better to walk through. Plant them on either side of a pathway and you can make a towering flower alley to impress your friends and family.

You will need

20 small plastic pots

potting mix

sunflower (*Helianthus annuus*) seeds

watering can with a fine rose

bricks or small stone slabs

small trowel

bamboo canes

garden twine or string

② On a patch of sunny ground, about 10 x 3ft (3 x 1m), place the bricks or small slabs on the ground to form a stepping-stone pathway. Alternatively, you can use an existing garden path that has flowerbeds on each side.

① Start off your sunflower seeds in small pots so that they can begin growing on a warm, sunny windowsill in spring. Fill each small pot with potting mix and firm this down. Make a small hole with your finger, about ¾in (2cm) deep, drop in a sunflower seed, and then cover over and firm down the potting mix before watering in well.

③ Once the sunflowers are about 8in (20cm) tall and all danger of frost has passed, you can plant them out. Make sure that the two lines of sunflowers on either side of the path are at least 3ft (1m) apart. This will give you enough room to run through them when they have grown. For each plant, dig a hole with the trowel about twice the size of its pot, carefully remove the plant, and put it in the hole, backfilling and firming the soil around it. Plant the next sunflower about 12in (30cm) further along and keep doing this until all of the sunflowers are planted. Remember to water the sunflowers in well.

④ When your sunflowers reach about 3ft (1m) in height, insert a bamboo cane next to each one and use the garden twine or string to tie the stem carefully to the cane in a figure-of-eight pattern. This will help to keep your sunflowers upright in strong winds. Loosen the ties as the stems get thicker so that they don't cut into them.

⑤ It is important to keep your sunflowers well watered, especially during hot, sunny spells. If you are going to be away, then ask a kind neighbor to water your sunflowers for you. When you come home, they will have grown even taller!

CHAPTER 5

Container Gardening

rain boot bulbs

If there's one thing guaranteed to grow faster than cress, it's children's feet. But old rain boots needn't be thrown away. Why not plant them with bulbs in the fall to make some colorful planters? Using three different types of bulb will give you weeks of color in the spring.

You will need

pair of old rain boots

warm soapy water

acrylic paint pens

clean gravel or small stones

potting mix

2 tulip (*Tulipa*) bulbs

2 daffodil (*Narcissus*) bulbs

8 crocus bulbs

(3) Put some potting mix on top of the gravel, making sure that you still have about a 6in- (15cm-) deep space for planting.

(1) Ask a grown-up to drill holes in an old pair of rain boots and then wash them on the outside with warm, soapy water. When they are dry, use the acrylic pens to decorate them with patterns, pictures, or even a special message.

(2) Fill the bottom "foot section" of the boot with gravel or small stones. This will help the boot stand up and also allow extra water to drain away after heavy rain or a good watering.

Try this... Rain boots make perfect pots for small plants. Try a bright red cyclamen for a winter rain boot decoration or pretty primroses for the spring.

4 Put in the tulip and daffodil bulbs, making sure that their pointed ends are upward. Cover these over with potting mix, leaving a 2in (5cm) gap at the top.

5 Plant the crocus bulbs, add more potting mix, and firm it down, making sure that it fills to just below the top of the boot. Plant up the other rain boot, water both boots well, and then put them somewhere sunny. Make sure that the potting mix doesn't get too dry.

spring basket

Old baskets can easily be lined to make perfect planters for a spring flower display, either to put on your own windowsill or as an Easter present for someone special. You can choose ribbons to coordinate with the color of your plants, as well as add other small decorations to brighten up the basket.

① Cut out a piece of plastic to line the wicker basket. Cut holes in the liner every 4in (10cm) and place it inside the basket.

② Fill the base of the lined basket with some gravel to help drainage. Add a layer of potting mix, firming it down as you go.

You will need

scissors

piece of plastic for the liner (e.g. an old potting-mix bag)

old wicker basket with a handle

gravel

potting mix

spring plants (e.g. hyacinths, miniature daffodils, primroses, and small-leaved ivies)

moss (real or sphagnum)

ribbons

small decorations, such as colored eggs or toy bunny rabbits

③ Carefully take your plants out of their pots and place them in the basket. When you are happy with how they look, add more potting mix around them to fill the basket to just below the rim. When you have finished planting, add sphagnum moss or real moss around the plants to create a lawn effect.

 Try this...thrift (charity) shops are great places to find old baskets.

④ Wrap a ribbon around the handle, leaving some extra lengths at both ends. Wrap a second ribbon around the handle in the other direction to make a pretty crisscross pattern, and again leave some lengths at the ends. Tie the two ribbon ends together to form bows at the bases of the handle.

⑤ Water the basket well outside, ensuring that any excess water has finished running out of the base before placing it on a windowsill. Finish off the planted basket with the decorations and then water carefully when needed, making sure you don't overwater.

mother's day teapot

Fresh mint tea is a refreshing drink and, with this clever teapot container, you can make sure your mother has a cup whenever she wants. If you can find a matching pitcher or sugar bowl, add a hand-picked posy and some tasty chocolates to make a whole tea tray of lovely gifts.

You will need
old teapot
gravel or small stones
potting mix
small mint plant
watering can

① Ask a grown-up to drill two to three holes in the base of an old teapot and place some gravel or small stones in the bottom to help with drainage.

② Add a handful or two of potting mix to the teapot before carefully taking the mint plant out of its pot. Be careful that you don't damage the roots of the plant when you do this.

③ Put the mint plant in the teapot, so that it is lined up with the top of the pot, and then carefully fill around it with more potting mix, firming it down as you do so.

Tip... Try to find a teapot that has a nice wide opening because this will make it easier to plant and also give more space for the mint leaves to grow.

④ Water the mint in well and then place the planted teapot on a sunny windowsill, watering when needed. You can then surprise your mother on Mother's Day.

wildflower bucket

Not many of us have room for a wildflower meadow, but how about having your own mini wildflower patch to carry around? This lovely bucketful of flowers will also attract lots of visiting insects to your garden to help pollinate fruit and vegetable plants.

You will need

plastic or metal bucket

gravel or large stones

potting mix

selection of annual wildflower seeds, such as corncockle (*Agrostemma githago*),

corn chamomile (*Anthemis arvensis*) and field cornflower (*Centaurea cyanus*)

small plate

watering can with a fine rose

① Ask a grown-up to puncture or drill several holes in the bottom of your bucket. Add some gravel or large stones to the bottom of the bucket to help with drainage.

② Fill the bucket with lots of potting mix, firming it down with your hands as you go. You may need to ask your grown-up to help you tip the heavy bag of potting mix into the bucket.

Put a selection of wildflower seeds on the small plate and mix them up with your finger. Sow the seeds by sprinkling them over the surface of the potting mix.

③ Gently sprinkle a little more of the potting mix over the top of the newly sown seeds, so they are just covered and no more.

Water the seeds in well before placing the bucket somewhere sunny. Remember to put a fine rose over the spout of your watering can so that you don't disturb the potting mix around the new seeds.

As the seeds grow, thin them out so that there is about 4in (10cm) between each plant. Thinning out in this way gives the new seedlings plenty of room in which to thrive and grow.

Try this... After the wildflowers have finished flowering, you can leave them to form seedheads. Then collect the seeds and keep them somewhere dry, dark, and cool ready for sowing the following year.

alpine wreath

Doors don't need to be dull. Use sempervivums in beautiful shades of purple, red, yellow, and green to make a living wreath that can decorate a garden shed or playhouse. If you haven't got an old wreath base to recycle, you can find them in florists' stores, large garden centers, or on online craft sites.

You will need

florists' plastic wreath ring base

potting mix

sempervivum plants

watering can

hammer and large nail

pretty ribbon and garden wire

1) Ask an adult to drill holes every 4in (10cm) in the bottom of the wreath ring base and fill with potting mix to just below the top.

2) Take the sempervivums out of their pots. If there are several sempervivums planted in one pot, then carefully break them up into individual plants.

3) Plant the largest sempervivums first, making a hole for their roots with your finger and pressing down the potting mix firmly around them when planted.

Try this... Sempervivums are succulent plants, which means that their leaves are cleverly adapted to withstand periods of dry weather. However, it is worth giving the wreath a good soaking every week to make sure it keeps growing.

④ Once the largest sempervivums have been planted around the ring base, use the smallest plants to fill in all of the gaps in between them.

⑤ When the ring is covered with plants, water well and then place it on a flat, sunny surface outdoors. Keep the ring watered in dry weather until the roots have started to grow again and are holding the plants securely in the ring (this usually takes about 3–4 weeks). Ask a grown-up to hammer a sturdy nail into a door from which you can hang your living wreath. Alternatively, suspend it using a pretty ribbon or a piece of garden wire.

edible flower colander

Surprise people twice over by using a kitchen colander as a planter and then filling it with flowers that you can eat! You can use edible nasturtiums and marigolds to brighten up all sorts of food. Why not try adding them to salads or sandwiches or even freezing the petals in ice-cube trays to bring color to summer drinks?

You will need

scissors

thick plastic bag, such as an old potting-mix bag

colander (larger sizes work best)

potting mix

1 pot marigold (*Calendula officinalis*)

2–3 nasturtiums (depending on the size of the colander)

watering can

1 Cut out a circle from the plastic bag, which is a little larger in diameter than the colander, and then carefully snip a few holes in the plastic with the pair of scissors.

2 Put the plastic circle inside the colander so that it is sitting centrally and then half-fill the colander with potting mix. Carefully trim away the excess plastic liner all around the top of the colander, but make sure that the liner covers the sides nicely all the way around.

Try this...Other good edible flowers that you might like to try growing in your colander include pansies and violets.

③ Gently remove the pot marigold from its container. You can do this easily by turning the pot upside down, while still supporting the plant with your fingers, and tapping the bottom of the pot until the plant comes out. Put the marigold in the center of the colander.

 Try this... Although you can buy nasturtiums and pot marigolds from the garden center, lots of gardeners grow them from seed first. For some helpful advice on growing plants from seed, see pages 8–10.

④ Remove the nasturtiums from their pots using the same technique as you did for the pot marigold, and then space them evenly around the edge of the colander.

⑤ Use some more of the potting mix to fill in the spaces between the pot marigold and the nasturtiums, firming down well as you go.

6 Water the plants in well. Place the colander somewhere relatively sunny and make sure that the potting mix doesn't dry out, especially in very hot weather. Remember that the best time to water your plants is either early in the morning or in the evening.

Try this...If you want to turn your colander into a hanging basket, simply tie a double length of garden twine or string around the neck of the colander and thread three evenly spaced pieces of twine under this to form the central hanger. Remember, the twine will snap if it is not replaced every few weeks. Also, to be safe, only hang the colander below head height.

miniature garden

You can make a miniature garden in all sorts of containers, as long as there are some holes in the bottom and you have enough room to be creative. This garden is made in a metal mixing bowl and uses lots of alpine plants, which are naturally tiny and so make perfect trees and bushes to decorate your miniature plot.

You will need

shallow metal mixing bowl, 10in (24cm) in diameter

gravel or small stones

potting mix

selection of alpine plants (e.g. *Hebe* 'Maori Gem', *H.* 'Green Globe' and *Sedum spathulifolium* 'Cape Blanco')

watering can

36 yellow Popsicle (lollipop) sticks

white (PVA) glue

25 green Popsicle (lollipop) sticks

scissors

card

short piece of string

thin twigs or canes

thin piece of material

mini card holders (for clothes pins)

thin sticks

baby sempervivums

moss (real or sisal)

small open shell

small pitcher

① Ask a grown-up to drill or puncture 5–6 holes in the base of your mixing bowl and then put a layer of gravel or small stones in the bottom to stop the potting mix blocking the holes. Add some potting mix and then place your alpine plants where you would like them to sit, allowing space for your path, shed, vegetable garden, and washing line. Fill around the plants with potting mix and give them a good watering.

② To make the sides of the shed, take the seven yellow sticks and carefully line them up. Cut another yellow stick so that it will fit across the first seven. Put a dab of glue on the two pieces of the last stick, lay them across the first seven sticks, and then place something heavy on top for about 20 minutes until they have stuck firmly. Repeat for the other side of the shed. To make the ends of the shed, repeat as for the sides but arrange the sticks so that they rise up to a point at the center.

③ Shorten three of the green sticks slightly with scissors and glue them onto the front of the shed to make a door. When fully dry, push all four sections into the potting mix so that they form the shed.

④ To make the roof, cut a square of card that is just larger than the top of the shed when it is bent in the middle. Cut ten green sticks so that they are slightly longer than one side of the card and stick them on using the glue. Repeat this for the other side.

⑤ Place the card on top of the shed, making sure that it is bent enough to be in line with the ends. Finally, stick on two sections of green sticks with glue, just slightly longer than the roof, to cover the spine of the card.

⑥ To make the gate, take another three yellow sticks and cut sections from a fourth to fit across the top and bottom, as well as diagonally across the middle. Stick these on using the glue. When it is dry, gently push the gate into position in the potting mix.

 Try this... You can use miniature furniture and figures or small toys to add more features to your garden.

7 To make the washing line, tie the piece of string to one end of two thin lengths of twig or cane. Push the twigs or canes into the potting mix so that the line is pulled taut. Cut a small piece of thin material to hang like washing on the line and attach it using the card pegs.

8 Break small sections of twig to form the edge of the path from the gate to the shed. Fill the central section with gravel.

9 Push in some thin sticks to make pretend supports for climbing beans and place the baby sempervivums in rows to look like cabbages or lettuces in the vegetable garden.

10 Fill around any bare areas with moss to look like grass. Add an upside-down shell to form a mini birdbath or small pond. Fill this carefully with water from a pitcher.

découpage pots

Black plastic plant pots may be useful, but they are not exactly works of art. Give them a colorful makeover using the ancient technique of découpage where you decorate the surface by sticking on paper cutouts. Suddenly, a dull pot becomes a homemade masterpiece worthy of the prettiest plants.

You will need

dish-cleaning brush

old plastic plant pot

warm, soapy water

selection of old wrapping paper

scissors

white (PVA) glue

water-based acrylic varnish

① Use the dish-cleaning brush to give the old plastic plant pot a good wash with warm, soapy water and leave it to dry.

② Choose a pretty piece of wrapping paper. Here, we have used some paper with a colorful cupcake pattern, but you can choose whatever design you like. Cut out your small pictures or shapes from the wrapping paper. The idea is to make your découpage pot as colorful and striking as possible.

③ Take the first picture, paste the back with the white (PVA) glue, and then stick it around the middle of the pot. Repeat this again and again, overlapping the pictures or shapes slightly each time so that none of the pot beneath is showing.

Try this... It is a nice idea to use different patterns and colors to complement whatever type of plant you are going to put in your pot.

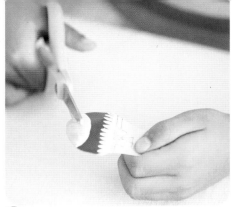

④ When you are ready to glue your shapes at the top or bottom of the pot, trim them down slightly before sticking them on so that the base and inside rim of the pot are not covered (these areas are more likely to get wet, which can damage the découpage pattern).

⑤ When all of the pictures and shapes have been glued onto your pot, apply 2–3 coats of water-based acrylic varnish to give your découpage some protection from water damage.

Templates

All the templates on this page are the correct size.
Simply trace them, then get crafting!

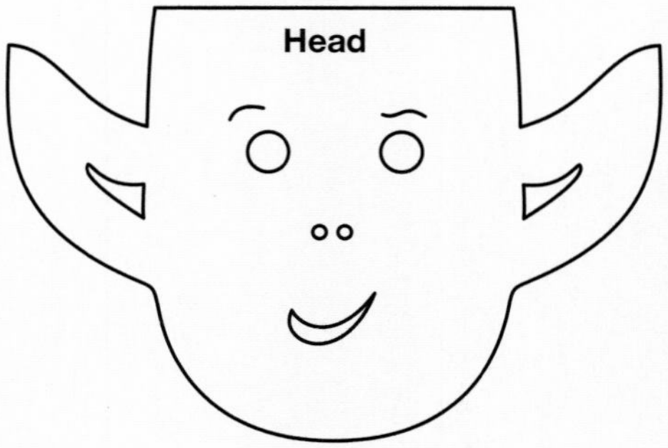

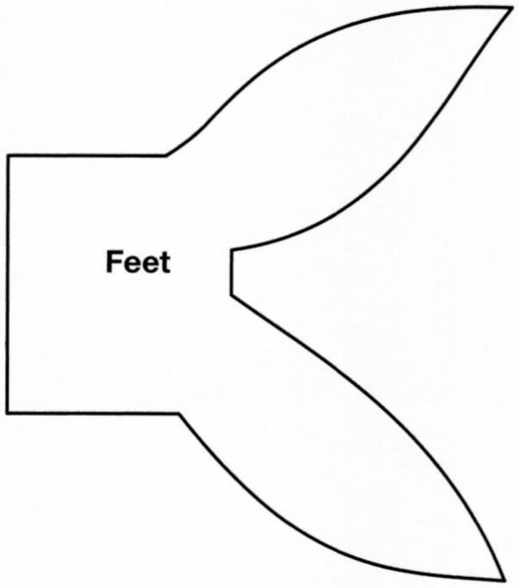

Head

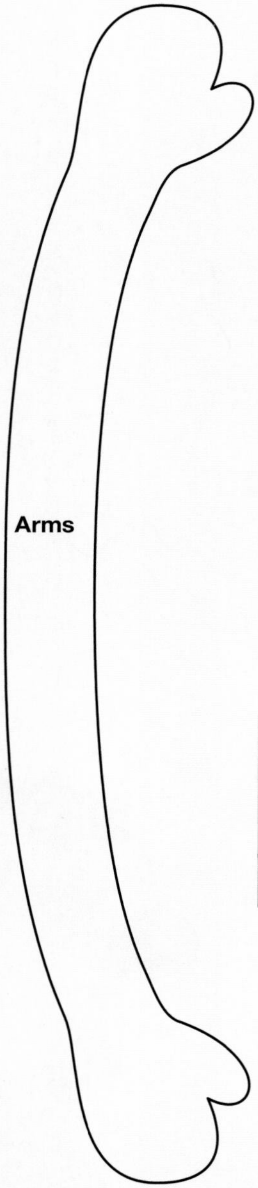

Bean

Arms

**CHRISTMAS GRASS
HEAD ELF** *page 23*

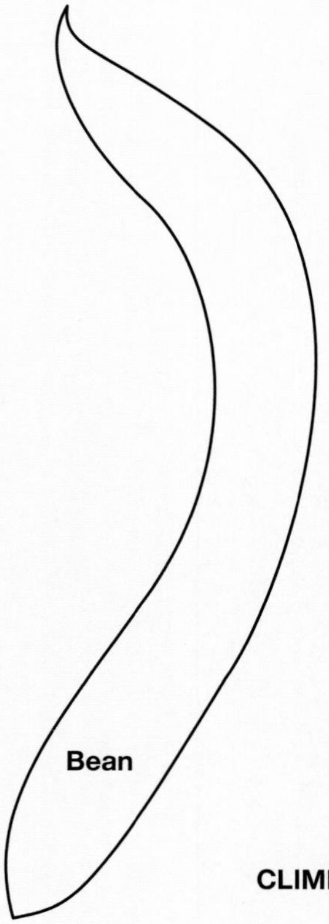

CLIMBING BEAN ARCHWAY
page 49

Feet

Leaf

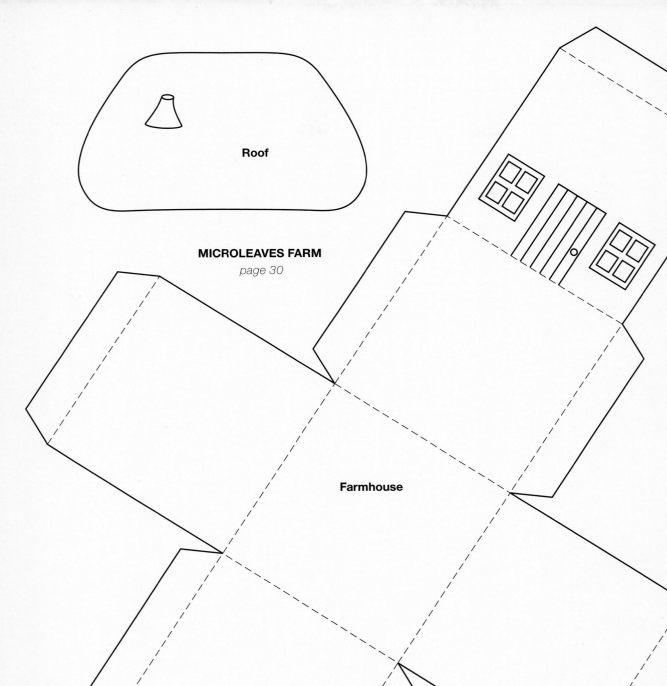

Roof

MICROLEAVES FARM
page 30

Farmhouse

Suppliers

Thrift stores / charity shops

Look in thrift stores (charity shops) for items such as old teapots, baskets, scarecrow outfits, and much more. Not only are these good value but the money you spend can help out people in need.

UK

Baker Ross

www.bakerross.co.uk
0844 576 8922
Huge range of craft accessories.

B&Q

www.diy.com
0845 609 6688
Wide selection of pots and trays. Also good for seeds, bulbs, gravel and grit, play sand, horticultural fleece, woodstains, masonry paint, broom handles, bamboo canes, twine, sandpaper, compost, straw and gardening tools.

Freecycle

This is a way to keep usable items out of landfill sites and is another great source of unwanted items, from old paving slabs to leaking wheelbarrows. Go to www.uk.freecycle.org.

Harrod Horticultural

www.harrodhorticultural.com
0845 402 5300
Good for children's gardening tools and clothes.

Hobbycraft

0845 051 6599
www.hobbycraft.co.uk
Massive range of craft materials online and instore from basic cards, papers, glues, and paints, to floral wreath rings, cookie cutters, silicon moulds, and flower presses.

Homebase

Covers a similar range of gardening and household goods as B&Q.

Homecrafts Direct

www.homecrafts.co.uk
0116 2697733
Online suppliers of a wide range of craft supplies.

Online Shells

www.onlineshells.co.uk
01785 661018
Suppliers of cockle shells.

Parkers

www.jparkers.co.uk
0161 848 1100
Good value source of mail order bulbs.

Wilkinsons

www.wilkinsonplus.com
08456 080807
Great source of good value household items and also has a craft range.

US

Craft Site Directory

Useful online resource
www.craftsitedirectory.com

Crafts etc.

800-888-0321
www.craftsetc.com

Create Kids Crafts

www.creativekidscrafts.com
510-364-2369

Hobby Lobby

www.hobbylobby.com
Stores nationwide

Kids Craft Supplies

www.kidscraftsupplies.com
866-777-8654

Michaels

www.michaels.com
Stores nationwide

S&S Worldwide Craft Supplies

www.ssww.com
800-288-9941

Index

Acknowledgments

Thank you to my publisher, CICO, and especially Cindy Richards, Sally Powell, Dawn Bates, and Caroline West for guiding me through this new world of book creation. Hats off to Emma Mitchell and Martin Norris for their brilliant photography and Sophie Martell, Emma Forge, and Elizabeth Healey for making it all look downright delicious. Also, my gratitude goes to my agent, Martine Carter, whose perseverance is legendary and without whom I would never have come this far.

To my truly super models Darcy, Maisie, Mia, Jamie, Elijah, Ellie, Daisy, and Tobias, I would like to say thank you for your patience and professionalism. And, most of all, to my three very gorgeous junior gardeners Ava, Oscar, and Archie, thanks for allowing me to brush your hair, put you in clean clothes and thrust you in front of a camera. I know at least two of these things go against your every instinct.

Finally, I must give special mention to my wonderful and long-suffering husband Reuben who has been unwavering in his support and who can, at long last, enjoy kitchen windowsills free of grass heads and bunny ears.